GREEN

AN ECLECTIC ANTHOLOGY OF
POETRY & PROSE

GREEN

An Eclectic Anthology of
Poetry & Prose

EDITED BY

MELANIE VILLINES

CONTRIBUTING EDITOR

JOAN JOBE SMITH

SILVER BIRCH PRESS

LOS ANGELES, CALIFORNIA, USA

ISBN-13: 978-0615758954
ISBN-10: 0615758959

FIRST EDITION, MARCH 2013

Email: silverbirchpress@yahoo.com
Web: silverbirchpress.com

Book Design: Silver Birch Press

The Silver Birch Press
GREEN ANTHOLOGY
is dedicated to
GRAHAM GREENE
(1904-1991)

INTRODUCTION

MELANIE VILLINES

Growing up in Chicago, one of the most anticipated events of the year occurred on St. Patrick's Day, when the Chicago River turned shamrock green. Whether we experienced the "Shannon River"—as the dyed waterway was dubbed for the day—from a downtown bridge, saw it on TV, read about it in the newspaper, or just heard about it from someone who was there, this annual happening was a magical moment that sparked the civic imagination.

I, for one, pictured myself floating down that green river to all kinds of fantastic places—the Emerald City and other amazing locales were around each bend.

Yes, the green river...the flow of imagination—that creative stream that artists ride and then return with the bounty. And, part of this bounty you're now reading—the Silver Birch Press *Green Anthology,* which contains creative explorations from authors in the U.S., U.K., Canada, Europe, and Africa. To all of our gifted contributors, thank you! A special note of gratitude and appreciation to contributing editor Joan Jobe Smith for bringing so many amazing authors into these pages.

For the *Green Anthology,* I've also selected green-related entries from past writing masters—including poets William Blake, Gerard Manley Hopkins, Amy Lowell, and Andrew Marvell, short story gurus Philip K. Dick and Kurt Vonnegut, legendary Irish novelist James Joyce, and revered children's book author L. Frank Baum. I've layered the work from today's writers with longstanding material from past writers to add interest and provide a sense of literary tradition.

In this collection—our sophomore voyage, following the Silver Birch Press *Silver Anthology* (Fall 2012)—we explore the many and varied connotations of the word "green": nature, the environment, money, envy, luck, seasons, flavors, food, and much more.

In these pages, you'll find poetry, short stories, novel excerpts, memoirs, fables, poetic essays, and several new features. With the *Green Anthology,* we're initiating author interviews, which we hope to include in subsequent anthologies. (Special thanks to Eddie Woods for allowing us to condense his 1982 interview with poet Jack Micheline and include it in this volume.) We've also added a new section entitled "Notes from the Authors," where contributors may offer insights into their work.

We dedicated the *Silver Anthology* to a man named Harold Martin Silver (aka Jack Micheline), so it seems fitting to dedicate the *Green Anthology* to someone named Greene. Graham Greene is considered by many as a writer's writer—and most authors I respect hold him in high regard. (Donna Hilbert's poem in this volume, "Seattle," expresses her esteem for the British author.)

I once sent a letter to Graham Greene in care of his publisher. The letter included a newspaper article about a politician who reminded me of a character in *Travels with My Aunt*, one of Greene's "entertainments," as he called them. A few months later, I received an envelope postmarked "Antibes"—and inside was a letter on beautiful monogrammed parchment from Greene's secretary thanking me for my letter and saying that the author was traveling at the moment. The envelope also included a large dead mosquito, which must have crawled inside during some point in the secretary's duties. I treasured this letter and kept it tucked inside a copy of Greene's spy novel, *The Third Man*. When I moved to Los Angeles, I ended up giving away most of my extensive library and this book and letter got misplaced in the mix and are now enjoying a second life somewhere.

A word on the layout...The *Silver Anthology* featured lightning on the cover and in a variety of lighting bolt photos inside the volume as a metaphor for inspiration. For the *Green Anthology*, the recurring image is clover. While researching this beautiful plant, I learned many interesting things, but my favorite was that it gives back more than it takes from the soil, and for this reason is considered an ideal plant.

In explaining my desire to create a themed anthology with recurrent imagery, I mentioned to a colleague recently that my esthetic preference was to look at one thing in many different ways. I also think the thematic resonance helps the component parts fit into some larger architecture in the reader's mind, making the material more meaningful.

So let's toast the Silver Birch Press *Green Anthology* with your favorite green beverage—whether it's a hearty brew, a bracing tea, a fizzy soda, or a shot of something stronger. Cheers!

Let's also celebrate the March 2013 release of the *Green Anthology* with a salute to the month's special occasions. Happy St. Patrick's Day, Happy Spring. Happy Passover and Easter! And happy one hundred and seventy-sixth birthday to the City of Chicago. Wishing all who read this boundless luck each and every day of the year.

TABLE OF CONTENTS

BARBARA ALFARO / 152

JENA ARDELL / 42, 158

AL BASILE / 109, 186, 230

L. FRANK BAUM / 52

WILLIAM BLAKE / 51, 239

JANE BUEL BRADLEY / 142, 227, 228

JOHN BRANTINGHAM / 240

JESSICA BROWN / 241

RACHEL CAREY / 25

CHRIS DAVIDSON / 35, 130, 156

PATRICK DELANEY / 119

COLLEEN DELEGAN / 101

PHILIP K. DICK / 144

BARBARA EKNOIAN / 118, 180, 208

DAN FANTE / 71

MERRILL FARNSWORTH / 66, 196, 197

SYED AFZAL HAIDER / 209

JOE HAKIM / 128, 184

HENRY VIII OF ENGLAND / 190

DONNA HILBERT / 73, 116, 229

GAIA HOLMES / 124, 134, 195

GERARD MANLEY HOPKINS / 115, 233

ZACK HUNTER / 63, 64

RODGER JACOBS / 107

JAMES JOYCE / 175

MICHAEL C. KEITH / 164

ERLE KELLY / 36, 226

RUTH MOON KEMPHER / 16, 17, 117

THOMAS KUDLA / 160

STEVEN KUHN / 15, 133, 236

MORIAH LaCHAPELL / 74

LEEANNE MCILROY LANGTON / 163, 203, 237

ELLARAINE LOCKIE / 78, 79, 80

GERALD LOCKLIN / 20, 50, 171

AMY LOWELL / 23, 125

SANDYLEE MACCOBY / 137

TAMARA MADISON / 18, 19, 45,

MARC MALANDRA / 44, 123, 223

KAREN MARGOLIS / 37, 39, 41

CLINT MARGRAVE / 166, 219

ANDREW MARVELL / 48

DANIEL MCGINN / 34, 201, 231

LORI MCGINN / 204, 220

MARCIA MEARA / 126

JACK MICHELINE / 22, 89, 93

BENJAMIN MYERS / 135, 234, 235

BROOKE NIA / 174, 181, 182

JAX NTP / 75, 76, 77

IVON PREFONTAINE / 131, 140, 141

JONNE RHODES / 240

CONRAD ROMO / 111

LUKE SALAZAR / 157

TERE SIEVERS / 13, 46, 215

JOAN JOBE SMITH / 198, 221

CLIFTON SNIDER / 70, 178, 214

DALE SPROWL / 14, 81, 207

KENDALL STEINLE / 193, 194, 216

TATE SWINDELL / 183

PAUL KAREEM TAYYAR / 54, 222, 243

G. MURRAY THOMAS / 21

JERI THOMPSON / 136

MARGARET TOWNER / 24, 205, 206

MARY UMANS / 30

DIRK VELVET / 43

PHILIP VERMAAS / 187

MELANIE VILLINES / 83

KURT VONNEGUT / 55

FRED VOSS / 199

BRUCE WEIGL / 169

TIM WELLS / 218

PAMELA MILLER WOOD / 192

EDDIE WOODS / 92, 93, 100, 151

NOTES FROM THE AUTHORS / 244

ABOUT THE AUTHORS / 248

SILVER BIRCH PRESS

GREEN ANTHOLOGY

PART	TITLE	PAGE
I	*HUES & FLAVORS*	12
II	*NATURE*	33
III	*EDEN*	47
IV	*DARK GREEN*	69
V	*MONEY*	106
VI	*WATER*	114
VII	*SEASONS*	132
VIII	*ENVY*	143
IX	*ENVIRONMENT*	155
X	*THE WORLD*	168
XI	*LOVE & MARRIAGE*	179
XII	*FAMILY*	202
XIII	*TREES*	225
XIV	*NEW LIFE*	238

PART I

HUES & FLAVORS

TERE SIEVERS

SHADES OF GREEN

Dusty taste of pistachio
summons the desert,
after the bite
green like the Palo Verde.
Creamy avocado
so smooth on the tongue,
soft in the hand but
hard in the heart.
A sting of Chartreuse
in a sip of the tongue,
burning bite from a bottle.
Now, breathe eucalyptus
inhale mint grass pine
swallow apple olive
drink in green.

Electric, asparagus, yellow, blue
forest, bright, marine and lime
Harlequin, honeydew, India, lawn
camouflage, citrine, emerald, jade
Paris, army, avocado, pear
verdigris, chlorine, office, sky
hunter, Persian, pigment, teal
turquoise, Kelly, moss and sap

Eucalyptus, grass, viridian, green.

DALE SPROWL

AQUA VITA

A color of aqua lives,
fantastically far from real;
Once I saw it behind Pablo Neruda's house
in a dream,
a stripe of Chilean ocean, cool and green.
Another time,
though this one real,
I saw it at the beach on Aruba,
Blown with racing winds,
sea over shallow white sand
pale as a pool.
Once I found it in nature
as I stared down at ice floes on Greenland,
white chunks cut into black lake,
each framed by numinous liquid refreshment.

And another time I saw it.
Would you call it real or not?
In Vincent's sky in *The White Orchard*.
When I saw it,
I wept,
uncontained,
until I saw it again in *The Plow*
and knew I was at home there.

STEVEN KUHN

GREEN

In the fall, green is weariness and dying,
but continues in the crack and shake of a glowstick
tied to a Halloween pail full of
brightly-colored wrappers.
Green shows best against black.
Now, and for a while, green must be manufactured.

Green is fragrant mint and teatree packaged in
green plastic tubes and
shampoo bottles—
the plastic plants in our living room fish tank,
or artificial trees, or a dead one, that improbably bring warmth
and something quiet into winter's whites and browns and grays.

In the spring, it is more genuine-
locust chirps, cicada underbrush,
the smell of sweat by river's edge, sticky,
insistent,
a reminder: we are not apart from nature.
Green is sex, not love.
Green is not patient.

Finally, in the summer, it's even
oppressive.
It bursts,
it is splendid,
and green becomes the first fireworks I ever saw,
blasting memory,
shimmering, percussive streaks of the novel new:
triumphant.

Ruth Moon Kempher

OF SEEING GREEN

"The mind. . .

Annihilating all that's made

To a green thought in a green shade."

Andrew Marvell, "The Garden"

The turn on is
modest green like
the Pharaoh's miasma
creeping in under the door

whose seeds
signal green, as
the issuing leaves will be
sunbuttered / greengroping creatures

jostled together
jolting cool static from each other—
a shock we might, accidentally, one day
between fragments of o'clock ourselves touch

whose need is glass green
as in tavern neon, or gumdrops
puddling on the floor. Spectral. No.
Wet. Like padded caterpillar feet. Green gore.

Originally published in *Casa de los Cinco Hermanos*
(Pueblo, Colorado)

Ruth Moon Kempher

HAZY AT THE MARKET

green tomatoes

forced in some flat
or with neon sunshine

not enough vitamins
to nourish the blight

wormless, of course
worms appreciate taste

why do I think of love
in connection with

packed in plastic, green
tomatoes? why am I faced

it is solid pulp and green
someone I could trust

vegetable connections
dreams: soft rain

Originally published in *Wormwood Review*

TAMARA MADISON

AVOCADOS

Shaped like tiny dinosaur eggs
with pebbly dark skin.
the little ones
are the most charming.

Slice through the creamy
green flesh
Remove the woody pit
and let it sit for a moment
in the palm of your hand

Imagine in this pit
the hum of life
before you drop it
into the trash.

Now draw lines
with your knife
across the smooth meat

Scoop the slices
out of the hardy brown skin

Mash them onto your toast
like thick green butter

This is the fat your body craves

As a child you hated them
but now you get it

It was one of those delicacies
that life was holding back—
a hidden pleasure
like sex, like alcohol
like bitter olives—

a new taste designed
to lighten
the dank and dripping pathways
of growing up.

TAMARA MADISON

FUGUE

On this fine autumn morning,

Bach knits a fugue around our home

in shades of red and rust,

earthen brown, deep forest green.

Corelli has filled our rooms

with flowers for Vivaldi to gild,

flinging his brush and spattering silver

and gold all over while Mozart

jumps up and down outside

on piles of fallen leaves shouting

"Look at me! Look at me!"

They'll keep this up forever,

while we at our breakfast table

with our coffee and our toast,

and all those things we've tried

so hard to make, will one day

be as gone as the crackling leaves

that gather on the lawn

and the wind that plays in the trees

a doleful variation in A.

GERALD LOCKLIN

GREEN CORN TAMALES

First in Tucson,
Now at El Cholo in L.A.
On Western just south of Olympic,
My wife and I make a point
Of enjoying them once a summer.

Some tamales are not hot.
These are sweet with the syrup
Of young corn, steamed within
The husks. Even the thin strand
Of a green pepper seems sweet.
Even the morsel of tender chicken
Seems sweet.

Sweet as sweethearts
On the evening promenade
Above the beach at Mazatlan.
Sweet as summer evenings.
Sweet as the respite, the
Renewal, at the end of day.

Think sweetly of green corn tamales,
Remembering that the water of the desert,
Hoarded by the thirsty cactus,
Is the sweetest water.

Reprinted by permission of the author from *The Life Force Poems,*
© Gerald Locklin, 2002, Water Row Press, Sudbury, Massachusetts.

G. Murray Thomas

GREEN

It was lime Lifesavers
that did it.
Yeah, lime Lifesavers.
Faced with the five colors—
red, orange, yellow, green and white—
Five flavors—
cherry, orange, lemon, lime and pineapple
(or was it grapefruit?)—
I chose lime.
And right then decided—
green was my favorite color.

This was the early 60s—
I was eight or nine—
long before "eco-awareness" entered anybody's awareness
—certainly not mine—
so that had nothing to do with it.
Also, despite the fact my parents were big campers,
and I spent much of my childhood outdoors
in the woods of upstate New York,
It had nothing to do with trees and leaves.
In fact, none of the associations we usually make about green—
nature, the environment, a soothing color, envy and the Irish—
had anything to do with it.

Although now I am Mr. Eco-Awareness,
and when I return to upstate New York
there is something, yes, soothing about all that rich foliage.
And so, even without the Irish (I'm more British in my lineage)—
and certainly without the envy—
Green is still my favorite color.

Sure, every now and then I flirt with purple
—especially rich, psychedelic purples—
and a hot pink can definitely catch my eye,
and certain blues have their charm—
like the golden blue of the ocean just as the sun sets,
and a rich aqua can definitely turn my head—
But aqua is really green, isn't it?
There you have it.
All because of lime Lifesavers.

JACK MICHELINE

GREEN

Green is the color of greed and grass and leaves of trees
Green eyes on witches and bitches
Green is the color of fields and mountains
Green is the color of Bukowski's rotting cheese
            in his icebox
Green is Ferlinghetti's hat and Bill Saroyan's chest
Green is the ring around Norman Mailer's face
Green is Janis Joplin's sky and breasts
Green is the color of Jack Kerouac's pea soup his
            mother made for him
Green are my gambler's pants
Green is the color of jade
Broccoli is green, spinach and peas are green
Snakes are green, Muldoon Elder is green, Charlie is green
Rasputin was red and green, red and green make brown
Green are the eyes of cats, emeralds, jade
Jungles are loaded with green
The Green Bay Packers are green
The Green Giant is green
The eyes of monsters are green
When my ass hurts it is green
Wall Street is green
Shamrocks are green
Saint Patrick's Day is a sea of green
The priests and nuns wave green
Green goes with red, blue and yellow and off-white
The sea is green
There are green hats, blouses, stockings, pants,
            and handbags
Green is a tough color
Stay away from green
It's the snot of your nostril
Beware of green guys with red hats
Currency is printed in green
Pirates wear green
The fields of the world are green, yellow, and blue
The sea is green,
A lush is green
Abundance is green
The frog is green, the fog is green
The world is loaded with green
The cat with green eyes danced up the street
Green, I love you green
            (*May 8, 1980, New York City*)

AMY LOWELL

INTERLUDE

When I have baked white cakes
And grated green almonds to spread upon them;
When I have picked the green crowns from the strawberries
And piled them, cone-pointed, in a blue and yellow platter;
When I have smoothed the seam of the linen I have been working;
What then?
Tomorrow it will be the same:
Cakes and strawberries,
And needles in and out of cloth.
If the sun is beautiful on bricks and pewter,
How much more beautiful is the moon,
Slanting down the gauffered branches of a plum-tree;
The moon,
Wavering across a bed of tulips;
The moon,
Still,
Upon your face.
You shine, Beloved,
You and the moon.
But which is the reflection?
The clock is striking eleven.
I think, when we have shut and barred the door,
The night will be dark
Outside.

MARGARET TOWNER

MY CELLS BEGIN TO SING

I feed my body

greens and fruit

berry and root.

A counterpoint balance

of grain and bean

that cross and twine.

Cells in perfect harmony

with earth and seed

sky and flower.

They find their

pitch and chord

rhythm and form

sing a symmetry

of nuclei and membrane

the heart and the whole

the mind and the soul.

Rachel Carey

DIRT

When Leo's mother got cancer, she told him she was going to a homeopathic healer. She didn't want to do chemotherapy, not if she wanted to stay in touch with the needs of her body, the wisdom of her own cells, her blood crying out for minerals that could only come from a leafy vegan diet. She had a list of herbs that would cure her. There was a woman in New Mexico who had gone into complete remission after taking Echinacea mixed with seaweed.

Leo told her that if she did that, she had only herself to blame if she died.

"I don't want to die. That's the whole point. Those doctors don't know me. They don't know my body."

"If you decide to kill yourself like this, I'm going to stop calling you, I swear. I mean it, Mom. You have to see a real doctor, and you have to do what he says."

"Leo," she said, "I love you very much, but you know nothing about the Earth."

They didn't talk for four months. Then in September, he flew out from Chicago on a Saturday morning and found her working at her food co-op. She had lost weight and her hands looked like bats' wings, strained and yellow. He was frightened. He apologized to her for running away from the situation. He said he'd been frightened. He coughed, waited as a customer came in and browsed the green tea selection, left again. She'd never heard him apologize before, and she felt sorry for him.

"Please let me take you to an oncologist. Please, Mom."

"I look like death, is that it?"

"I didn't say that."

She sighed, looked at the long row of herbal medicines on the far wall, and said she would go, but it had to be a woman doctor, and she wouldn't promise she'd comply with any instructions.

Four days later, after their first visit to a local oncologist, Leo sat in his mother's living room while she cooked them dinner. It was the apartment he'd grown up in, on the first floor of a broad Victorian three-family in the rolling hills of Portland, Maine. It was an artistic neighborhood, where people made their own pottery and painted colorful signs with the names of their stores. As a teenager, he'd wanted nothing more than to leave.

Now he sat staring at the collection of quartz crystals and sea glass on the side table. How he had loved it all, once. Her beautiful knick-knacks. As a child, he had believed in their mystical properties, as she had. He still had a single, vibrant image of her burned in his head from those days. He must have been about six years old, and his mother was standing a few feet from him on the beach, looking at the ocean with a guitar over her shoulders, her hair flying in the wind at sunset, her long silver skirt blown back, eyes shut, playing one chord after another as the melody got lost in the sound of the sea. She had believed in the natural world back then, and he had felt her to be imbued with mystical power, a queen of the fairies, capable of healing any wound.

That had changed with the divorce. It wasn't that his father had been a major presence in his early life, but when his mother finally moved them out of his father's house in semi-industrial Bath and into their new place in Portland, Leo's blind faith in his mother began to wane. He was nine, and could suddenly see the hocus-pocus nonsense of her New Agey music, her circle of chattering friends, her yoga mantras. "My aura." "Female intuition." "Inner light." Was "inner light" what had led her to walk out on his dad? And for what, a drafty house, a car that was usually broken? Sometimes there were moths in the granola, and she'd say, "It adds protein."

At sixteen, he'd left and moved in with his father, worked in his dad's garage until his father told him not to work in a goddamn garage all his life. He reluctantly agreed to take a few classes at the local community college, planning to drop out, but the rigor of his science classes had pleased him. Here, at last, was truth. So he had stayed and eventually transferred to a better school, and then on to a master's degree in chemistry.

He became a medical researcher and began working in various research labs. He was an expert at setting up clean rooms, a master of lab protocol, and he spent half his life in white full-body clean suits, every skin cell a potential contaminant. It was nice, though his mother was horrified. Everything seemed so solid and verifiable. Every experiment was a reliable data point, so long as you could keep out the dirt.

Still, his father had died of heart disease at fifty-six, and science couldn't save him. And now his mother had no interest in medicine at all.

"I want to be buried on a hillside overlooking the sea," she said as she walked out of the kitchen and put a plate of lentil and red pepper soup at his regular old place at the table.

"What are you talking about?" he said. "It's not too late, now that you've started to see a real doctor."

"You weren't listening to her today," she said.

"She said fifty-fifty."

"There's a place in South Portland I think might be nice."

He hated her for that, too. What did it matter where she was buried? She wouldn't be there to see the sea. All it did was guarantee that she would be nowhere near Chicago, that he would never be able to visit her grave. But when she died the next June, he obliged her anyway. Her body was placed in an old nineteenth century cemetery, on a long sloping hill overlooking the harbor.

When he returned to her house after the funeral, he saw her ancient rust-brown Nissan sitting in the driveway with a "Go Green" bumper sticker slowly peeling away, and he stared at it for a long moment before angrily peeling it away. When he went into the house to pack up her clothes, he found her old silver skirt and started crying.

The following June, he got sick.

"The anniversary of your mother's death," said Dawn, the fat, earnest receptionist at his research lab. "Perhaps your body is reacting to that." He dismissed this as junk science. His problem was intestinal, a constant misery in his gut, an aching exhaustion, diarrhea. An emotional disorder would have taken a more romantic form, surely, like tuberculosis or suicide.

All the same, her comment bothered him. Was this guilt? Guilt that he hadn't seen his mother, that he'd visited her so little? Guilt about those four months when he could have saved her, had he turned up earlier, convinced her earlier? He'd flown out once a month for her final six months. Wasn't that enough? Should he have quit his job? He'd invited her to live with him, and she'd declined. What else was he supposed to do?

He was relieved when his doctor told him that his illness had a name. *Clostridium difficile.* A bacterial infection. He'd taken some antibiotics for a brief bout of strep throat, and the bacterium must have taken hold in his weakened gut. He learned that fourteen thousand Americans died of the disease every year.

This at least gave him something to work on. He took antibiotics again, trying to destroy the infection, but the problem returned. Worse this time. So he looked up the best names in the field, which people were working on this, what were they doing, who were the experts, who knew the facts.

This was how he found himself sitting on the examining table of Dr. Angela Murray, Harvard Medical School, University of Chicago Residency. Her bedside manner was a little too nurturing for Leo's taste, but he listened carefully when she sat down on the stool opposite him.

"We've discovered in the last few decades that the body is its own little ecosystem. When you're a toddler, you put all kinds of things in your mouth and you end up eating a lot of dirt and getting exposed to bacteria and stuff in your environment, and you drink breast milk, and your intestinal track gets primed with the right bacteria, and your body gets adjusted. There's even some evidence that intestinal parasites can serve a helpful function as an anti-inflammatory. But now people get sick, they take antibiotics, and they kill the good stuff in their system along with the bad. What we've got to do is repopulate your inner ecosystem, Leo."

She gave him a list of probiotics to start eating. Yogurt. Kimchi. "There's no guarantee any of this will work, but we've got to get some of the right bacteria back into you. It's the best shot we have."

It didn't work, of course. He'd been certain it wouldn't. The body wasn't an ecosystem; it was a machine. Six weeks later, he found himself lying on the bathroom floor one morning, immobile, exhausted, unable to rise to even call for help for over forty minutes. So after visiting the E.R. he tried another doctor—a man, more practical, no talk of ecosystems.

Antibiotics again. Another regimen. It was risky. It could make the problem worse. He tried it. The bacteria returned.

He began to fear, in a vague way, that he might be dying.

He'd never had children. He'd never contributed in that way to the ecosystem of the world. He had not cured some famous disease, though he'd nudged knowledge forward here and there in a small corner of his field. Facing the real prospect of his death, alone, without a spouse or anybody to care for him, he came to realize that he'd been carefully ignoring that he was a part of a whole earth, of the human community. He had spent the bulk of his life in cold, white, clean rooms. He was a living thing, and he had forgotten to remember that. He wondered if this was the knowledge that his mother had been playing into the ocean with her guitar that day.

He took a week of medical leave from work and got on a plane and flew to Portland, one last time. His stomach was sick the whole way, he had to use the bathroom four times on the plane ride, and was sick in a rental car. There was no way to explain it, no way to talk about it, how feeling sick like that made you just want to die. Perhaps his mother had known that at the end, too. Perhaps her feelings had been similar to his.

Repopulation of his gut. He thought of picking up toys as a small child, shoving dirt into his mouth. It was absurd that those foolish, unsanitary actions could set up a whole lifetime of well-being, and that a foolish adult could undo that somehow.

It was April, and his mother's grave was thick with spring grass. It was too early for lupine season, but the other wildflowers were in bloom at the edges of the cemetery, and the hillside was a carpet of green. He sat down on his mother's grave, on her lap, like the little boy he had once been.

"You know nothing about the Earth, Leo." He wondered what bacteria were around him now. Perhaps the right ones, the good ones, the very ones that he'd eaten as a tiny boy. Perhaps if he could eat just the right thing, his intestines would repopulate, his life would be saved.

He knew it was foolish, but he scratched one fingernail across the fresh brown soil and moved the finger to his lips, looking around to see if anyone could see him, and then placed it in his mouth and tasted the sweet, ancient flavor of the dirt.

MARY UMANS

THE ALPHABET OF GREEN
with Footnotes

I have a hybrid I'm driving green
Soon I'm driving to *A*bilene.

I eat vegetables that are green
But I won't eat a lima *B*ean.

I was swimming and my hair turned green
I think there was too much *C*hlorine.

The school colors are purple and green
You'd think he'd wear them, he's the *D*ean.

I think I'm innocent, fresh, still green
I'm not old, just an *E*x-teen.

Blue and yellow make the color green
Blue like sky, yellow like *F*luorine[1]

Drive electric and you'll be green
Your car will use no *G*asoline

Christmas colors are red and green
Not orange and black like *H*alloween.

Teal and turquoise aren't blue or green
Both are colors *I*n-between.

---

[1] Fluorine is a toxic yellowish gas. Fluorine is used in rocket fuel, refrigerators and toothpaste.

On St. Pat's we all wear green
Patty, Mario, and *J*oaquin.

If you like walking in fields of green
Don't go hiking around Loch *K*atrine.[2]

Olive drab is military green
The military bathroom is *L*atrine.

The Incredible Hulk is big and Green
A big, fierce, fighting *M*achine.

I'm so jealous, I turn green
Whenever I see pretty *N*oreen.

Now I'm drinking tea that's green
As a kid I drank *O*valtine.[3]

Veggies are good, eat the green
But be sure to get enough *P*rotein.

Money, money, I want the green
I want to live just like the *Q*ueen.

Mondays I shop and I shop green
I bring my own bag, that's my *R*outine.

Actors wait in a room called green
Before going on stage to act their *S*cene.

➤

---

[2] Loch Katrine is a freshwater loch in Scotland made famous in Sir Walter Scott's poem, "The Lady of the Lake" in 1810.

[3] Ovaltine is a chocolate milk powder.

It's pea soup that's why it's green
It's sitting in a soup Tureen.
So many uses for the word green
I would say there are Umpteen. [4]

The U.K. has a book call Green
Updating professionals on Vaccine. [5]

Michigan State colors are white and green
Not the blue and maize of the Wolverine. [6]

The mutant ninja turtles are all green
Their power must come from the X-gene. [7]

Ireland is an isle of green
With pastures for sheep, their lambs to Yean. [8]

I'm in an anthology of green
More traditional than a homemade Zine. [9]

---

[4] Umpteen stands for an indefinite number.

[5] The *Green Book* put out by the U.K. gives the latest vaccines and vaccination procedures for all the vaccine-preventable infectious diseases that may occur in the U.K.

[6] Wolverine is the nickname for the University of Michigan.

[7] The x-gene is the DNA complex responsible for the superpower of mutants according to Marvel comics.

[8] To yean means to bring forth young when speaking of sheep or goats.

[9] 'Zine is most commonly a homemade or online often underground publication.

PART II

NATURE

DANIEL MCGINN

OUTSIDE

Walking down the narrow trail
into the shadow canyon,
a red-tailed hawk with wings spread
was gliding overhead, when she said,
That's what we need, clear oxygen.

And that's what we'd been missing.
Walking helps me remember.
I remember when we could see the stars
all night long if we wanted to

or papoose the twins and walk
up Cow Mountain
if we wanted to.

I remember driving slow down Talmage Road
that autumn, when the grape leaves were turning
the color of wine, nobody but us taking that road
and we could drive as slow as we wanted to.

I remember red clay sticking to my boots
as we walked the trails on the Greenwood Ridge,
the way those mountains talked to us,
and emptied us, and filled us.

There is nothing like the cool green air
in my nose, in my ears,
deep in the hollow,
just past the ferns.

CHRIS DAVIDSON

I WAS IN PISMO BEACH

I was in Pismo Beach with my wife
and her mother Phyllis and her husband Greg,
and we stayed in a hotel room on the second floor,
with two queen-sized beds,
and Greg stood by the open door of the room,
smoking, looking out at the ocean, where he saw,
under thick white clouds lumbering cross the sky
like whales, whales—first time he'd seen them
in the wild, he said. And the smoke lifted
from his cigarette, and the mist from the whales
lifted as if in reply, and all of this
I don't remember, none of it, not the trip
to Pismo Beach, not the whales,
but Phyllis does, for she talked about it
here when she came to visit last week.
My wife barely recalls it, *sort of* is
the phrase she uses. All was recounted
as we walked on a pier at a different beach—
myself, my wife, and Phyllis, who pushed
her grandchildren in the stroller, the sound
of water below bringing up the hotel, the smoke,
the whales and waves, whatever else.

ERLE KELLY

THE HUMMINGBIRD NEST

Her morning starts long before mine.
I look out the window for progress.
There it is, without mom, molded
into the vertex of two twigs
partly camouflaged by leaves.
The circumference of a quarter,
the mossy green and grey-white nest
complements the mother's colors.
Suddenly she flies in, hovers
with a feathery remnant and places
it on the nest wall that holds
the aspirin-sized white egg
barely visible at the bottom.
She fluffs her body over the crib,
mother and nest melt into the green
and ride the wave of wind
between the house and row of ficus.

KAREN MARGOLIS

I am a hill of poetry

on the birth of Quila Lulu Anastasia
14 January 1995

I am a hill of poetry
my tip houses an eagle's nest
where dreams hatch into song
my base flows into the well of life
to join the subterranean rivers
in caves that echo with the playing of a dulcimer;
my belly is filled with the runes of ages
and the hand of the bard strokes my mound
like a mother caressing the head of her infant child.
Precious ores run in my deepest veins
mingling with the pulsing rhythms of the earth
in lustrous ecstasy. Rhymes
flick their tongues from the mouths of lizards
lying sundrenched in my surface crannies.
In summer grass covers my gentle slopes,
in autumn the tree gods shower me with colour,
in winter my thoughts are naked, unashamed,
and when the year wakes to spring again
I'm still there, breeding lilacs and hexameters

I am a hill of poetry.
Enter my gates carved by the singers of psalms
to let in the light at the winter solstice.
Crawl through the tunnel maze to my ancient mystery:
the journey is long and hard
the rebirth into poetry is spiked with pain
and promises only rediscovery
of what life takes away
each day we grow farther from childhood.

I am a hill of poetry.
Come inside me. All my passages spread out
like starry beams. In my hollow core
bowls of incense fill the air with perfume
a bed of feathers is waiting for your weary tune.
Lie down. Close your eyes.

➤

Shut out straying conversations.
Drift on a tide of rapturous melancholy
down to castles hung with tapestries
where troubadors tell tales of victories;
weave the stuff that dreams are made of
with the words that flood your mind
press them between the pages of a book
that closes only at the edge of time.

I am a hill of poetry.
I stand here by the grace of nature.
One day the earth will open up and swallow me
into the canyons of desire.

KAREN MARGOLIS

I am a stag of seven tines

for TSch...

I am a stag of seven tines
see how my regal antlers reach
in fourteen spears of pride toward the sun
as it climbs from the dark midwinter mists
stretching the days since the narrow light beam
pierced to the bowels of the rath, the sleepers' tomb
where druids and warriors curl up to dream
while curved shields stand guard for the white goddess.

At break of day they come to hunt me down
men of the age of stone, blue their eyes
like cornflowers in the field, seeking my sight
as I turn my head to the cold grey sky; pale faces
ashen as the chalk upon their ox-hide shields;
golden manes lapping their shoulders
like ebbtide on the shores where the sons of Mil
landed from the east to win a continent,
and sailors driven by the wild winds of the sea
returned with stories of a newfound world
beyond the west horizon.   Hot from the chase
men dance toward me, nostrils quivering
at the scent of potency, weapons raised to kill
casting shadows on the hills where poets walk.

I am a stag of seven tines.
Listen to the roar of the leaves
as I break through into the clearing.
The hunters pause for breath. Their feet
can never catch the rhythm of my racing flight.
I find the birch tree that watched over my birth —
horn to bark, we rub our past into fresh beginnings.

Now I am an ox of seven fights.
Feel my taut muscles beneath my coat
firm to the touch. My twin-pointed crown
is borrowed by pharaohs and monstrous beasts.

➤

In the depths of the forest by the ring of stones
I turn to face a man who wants my flesh to eat
and my skin to protect the secrets of his body.

I am an ox of seven fights.
Once I shared a stall with the kingly stag.
My blood, painted long ago on the walls of caves
Shall picture life to coming generations.

KAREN MARGOLIS

I am a threatening noise of the sea

for Solomon David Margolis
born 22 November 1927, died 23 May 2003

I am a threatening noise of the sea
prophesying the fall of tyranny
as the last leaves drop from the trees
and the first frost creeps on the ground with spiders' legs.
On the Atlantic seaboard I throw pebbles to their fate
beating out the rhythm of the wind
that whistles through reed beds of Egyptian rivers.
At night the screech owl joins our savage song.

I am a threatening noise of the sea
echoing the thunder of the world beneath the waves,
summoning the year's seven proudest beauties
to suck the garnet fruits of paradise;
they spit the chewed-up seeds of cooling passion
(the taste of summer lingers on their tongues),
then dance slow motion round the fires of wisdom
in the realm of the goddess who lusts for darkness
—in the late afternoon she swallows the sun.

Mine is the season of commemoration:
The unknown soldier gets his yearly wreath.
Mine the festival of lonely and departed souls
and the moment of abandoned revolutions
when history's scorpion stings the feet of change.
My nights slip into murky fog pyjamas
and fold themselves round every living thing.
My days arise in glittering morning gowns—
We all reach winter even if we dread it.

I am a threatening noise of the sea
A king of infinite sound, mocking the silence of the snow.
Before I surrender my sceptre to the deep
I'll take my bow and shoot my twelve straight arrows
Like rays into the rooftop of the sky.

JENA ARDELL

SPRING SINGS IN ME

The sparrows
are shining from the rain,
twitter as they
go by.
I could not be so
bare and brown
And fly,
little clouds
with a windy April grace

With only one unchanging tree—
Spring sings in me.

DIRK VELVET

OKAUCHEE

The
Blue Jays
woke us
at dawn
with their
jeering
calling to the cottage
from
weeping willows
whose roots
reached as far into the lake
as onto the land
The water was
cool green
at its best
and gray-black at its worst
Okauchee
nothing else mattered
Not
tangling weeds
floating fish
sinking rafts
Okauchee
it was all we ever knew
or
wanted
of summer
At dusk we piled into the attic
strewed across mattresses
no longer wanted at home
we listened to
the bats chatter
as it lulled us
to
sleep
      (Okauchee Lake. Okauchee, Wisconsin)

MARC MALANDRA

CHASING RAVENS FROM MY ROOF

On this day of odd foreboding
the crows have brought me
what they would not bring Noah:

a twig from grief's green field,
an opportunity to turn dark
thoughts into birds I chase away,

a chance to open the brain's cage
wide enough to let in one poem while
a dozen noisy reminders of everything

I'm not nor ever shall be rises up, cawing
vainly at my power to make them leave,
a power that erases black ink

blotches that have fallen across
the letter I write myself, journal
entry corpse doomed to a coffin—

drawer no one will ever open. And
even as I contemplate the power
I have over these birds I see

they have not perched far off,
waiting for another chance to pluck
hope from my furrowed brow.

TAMARA MADISON

THE RAPTURE

How I envy
the furry black
yellow striped
caterpillar
that climbs
the lush stems
of the basil plant.
Sheltered within the deep
green redolent canopy
it spends its days
feasting
on the fragrant leaves,
unaware
that with each
delicious bite
it destroys
its gorgeous habitat.
By the time the leaves
are all reduced
to lacy stubble
it will be time
to find a resting place,
pull a cocoon over itself
and wait for the dawn
of the next life.
How I envy
the furry black
yellow striped
caterpillar
that can destroy
its world
and retreat
to the succor
of a regenerative
cocoon.

TERE SIEVERS

MONARCH

Black antennas twitch
as the caterpillar
strips the last green leaf
from the naked milkweed.
Striped flesh shed,
green skin below
becomes
a gold-rimmed jade pendant
hung by a black thread.
Nature, that green magician,
arranges a sleight of hand.
The fat worm in a striped suit
slides into its chrysalis
naps for a fortnight
wakes,
draped in orange
ready to dance.

PART III

EDEN

ANDREW MARVELL

THE GARDEN

How vainly men themselves amaze
To win the palm, the oak, or bays,
And their uncessant labours see
Crown'd from some single herb or tree,
Whose short and narrow verged shade
Does prudently their toils upbraid;
While all flow'rs and all trees do close
To weave the garlands of repose.

Fair Quiet, have I found thee here,
And Innocence, thy sister dear!
Mistaken long, I sought you then
In busy companies of men;
Your sacred plants, if here below,
Only among the plants will grow.
Society is all but rude,
To this delicious solitude.

No white nor red was ever seen
So am'rous as this lovely green.
Fond lovers, cruel as their flame,
Cut in these trees their mistress' name;
Little, alas, they know or heed
How far these beauties hers exceed!
Fair trees! wheres'e'er your barks I wound,
No name shall but your own be found.

When we have run our passion's heat,
Love hither makes his best retreat.
The gods, that mortal beauty chase,
Still in a tree did end their race:
Apollo hunted Daphne so,
Only that she might laurel grow;
And Pan did after Syrinx speed,
Not as a nymph, but for a reed.

What wond'rous life in this I lead!
Ripe apples drop about my head;

The luscious clusters of the vine
Upon my mouth do crush their wine;
The nectarine and curious peach
Into my hands themselves do reach;
Stumbling on melons as I pass,
Ensnar'd with flow'rs, I fall on grass.

Meanwhile the mind, from pleasure less,
Withdraws into its happiness;
The mind, that ocean where each kind
Does straight its own resemblance find,
Yet it creates, transcending these,
Far other worlds, and other seas;
Annihilating all that's made
To a green thought in a green shade.

Here at the fountain's sliding foot,
Or at some fruit tree's mossy root,
Casting the body's vest aside,
My soul into the boughs does glide;
There like a bird it sits and sings,
Then whets, and combs its silver wings;
And, till prepar'd for longer flight,
Waves in its plumes the various light.

Such was that happy garden-state,
While man there walk'd without a mate;
After a place so pure and sweet,
   What other help could yet be meet!
But 'twas beyond a mortal's share
To wander solitary there:
Two paradises 'twere in one
To live in paradise alone.

How well the skillful gard'ner drew
Of flow'rs and herbs this dial new,
Where from above the milder sun
Does through a fragrant zodiac run;
And as it works, th' industrious bee
Computes its time as well as we.
How could such sweet and wholesome hours
Be reckon'd but with herbs and flow'rs!

GERALD LOCKLIN

A GREEN THOUGHT?

Andrew Marvell is best known for
His seductively detailed, syllogistically argued
Plea "To His Coy Mistress,"
The Carpe Diem to end all Carpe Diems.
But in graduate school we were instructed
To appreciate as well the elusive, ineluctable
Analyses of Mind (Human and or Universal?)
That constitute this polar removal from the External,
Or Mirror of It: "The Garden." And to admire it
As including perhaps the most musically
Beautiful and enigmatic couplet in English Verse:
"Annihilating all that's made
To a green thought in a green shade."

Ever the pedagogue, I'll suggest the poem
Anticipates by two centuries the "*ineffable,*"
And the "correspondences" between the Visible World
And the Ocean of Thought of the French Symbolists—
Nerval, Baudelaire, Verlaine, Rimbaud, Mallarmé, Laforgue,
Corbière, Valéry, and, arguably, Apollinaire,
And of our own Edgar Allan Poe, T. S. Eliot,
Hart Crane, and Wallace Stevens, not to mention,
A sequence of major, cross-disciplinary movements
That partially derived from them: Futurism, Dadaism,
Surrealism (Freudian, then Marxist), and
L-A-N-G-U-A-G-E.

But, like a lazy Socrates, I'll also let you
Discover or Revisit for yourselves the Many Mansions
Of this philosophical inquiry in nine stanzas
Of eight lines of four stresses each,
Into the nature of the consciousness
And of the Green World which may exist either
Within it or outside it or as simply with it:
A single Green Thought in a Green Shade,
Or a Boundless Master-Matrix-Molecule of Many.

WILLIAM BLAKE

LAUGHING SONG

When the green woods laugh with the voice of joy,
And the dimpling stream runs laughing by;
When the air does laugh with our merry wit,
And the green hill laughs with the noise of it;

When the meadows laugh with lively green,
And the grasshopper laughs in the merry scene,
When Mary and Susan and Emily
With their sweet round mouths sing "Ha, ha he!"

When the painted birds laugh in the shade,
Where our table with cherries and nuts is spread:
Come live, and be merry, and join with me,
To sing the sweet chorus of "Ha, ha, he!"

L. FRANK BAUM

THE EMERALD CITY OF OZ

EXCERPTS

The Emerald City is built all of beautiful marbles in which are set a profusion of emeralds, every one exquisitely cut and of very great size.

There are other jewels used in the decorations inside the houses and palaces, such as rubies, diamonds, sapphires, amethysts and turquoises.

But in the streets and upon the outside of the buildings only emeralds appear, from which circumstance the place is named the Emerald City of Oz. It has nine thousand, six hundred and fifty-four buildings, in which lived fifty-seven thousand three hundred and eighteen people, up to the time my story opens.

All the surrounding country, extending to the borders of the desert, which enclosed it upon every side, was full of pretty and comfortable farmhouses, in which resided those inhabitants of Oz who preferred country to city life.

Altogether there were more than half a million people in the Land of Oz—although some of them, as you will soon learn, were not made of flesh and blood as we are—and every inhabitant of that favored country was happy and prosperous.

⌘

For some time Ozma has ruled over this fair country, and never was Ruler more popular or beloved. She is said to be the most beautiful girl the world has ever known, and her heart and mind are as lovely as her person.

Dorothy Gale had several times visited the Emerald City and experienced adventures in the Land of Oz, so that she and Ozma had now become firm friends. The girl Ruler had even made Dorothy a Princess of Oz, and had often implored her to come to Ozma's stately palace and live there always; but Dorothy had been loyal to her Aunt Em and Uncle Henry, who had cared for her since she was a baby, and she had refused to leave them because she knew they would be lonely without her.

However, Dorothy now realized that things were going to be different with her uncle and aunt from this time forth, so after giving the matter deep thought she decided to ask Ozma to grant her a very great favor.

A few seconds after she had made the secret signal in her little bed-chamber, the Kansas girl was seated in a lovely room in Ozma's palace in the Emerald City of Oz. When the first loving kisses and embraces had been exchanged, the fair Ruler inquired:

"What is the matter, dear? I know something unpleasant has happened to you, for your face was very sober when I saw it in my Magic Picture. And whenever you signal me to transport you to this safe place, where you are always welcome, I know you are in danger or in trouble."

Dorothy sighed.

"This time, Ozma, it isn't I," she replied. "But it's worse, I guess, for Uncle Henry and Aunt Em are in a heap of trouble, and there seems no way for them to get out of it—anyhow, not while they live in Kansas."

"Tell me about it, Dorothy," said Ozma, with ready sympathy.

"Why, you see Uncle Henry is poor; for the farm in Kansas doesn't 'mount to much, as farms go. So one day Uncle Henry borrowed some money, and wrote a letter saying that if he didn't pay the money back they could take his farm for pay. 'Course he 'spected to pay by making money from the farm, but he just couldn't. An' so they're going to take the farm, and Uncle Henry and Aunt Em won't have any place to live. They're pretty old to do much hard work, Ozma; so I'll have to work for them, unless—"

Ozma had been thoughtful during the story, but now she smiled and pressed her little friend's hand.

"Unless what, dear?" she asked.

Dorothy hesitated, because her request meant so much to them all.

"Well," said she, "I'd like to live here in the Land of Oz, where you've often 'vited me to live. But I can't, you know, unless Uncle Henry and Aunt Em could live here too."

"Of course not," exclaimed the Ruler of Oz, laughing gaily. "So, in order to get you, little friend, we must invite your Uncle and Aunt to live in Oz, also."

"Oh, will you, Ozma?" cried Dorothy, clasping her chubby little hands eagerly. "Will you bring them here with the Magic Belt, and give them a nice little farm in the Munchkin Country, or the Winkie Country—or some other place?"

"To be sure," answered Ozma, full of joy at the chance to please her little friend. "I have long been thinking of this very thing, Dorothy dear, and often I have had it in my mind to propose it to you. I am sure your uncle and aunt must be good and worthy people, or you would not love them so much; and for your friends, Princess, there is always room in the Land of Oz."

Paul Kareem Tayyar

AT YOSEMITE

I was nineteen,

And the waterfall looked to me like something that only existed in Avalon,

In Camelot,

In an Eden where green apples were plucked and devoured without consequence,

Where the lovers' nakedness only made them love each other more,

Where they slept beneath skies so wide at night that not even God's arms

     Could reach all the way across

When I leapt from one rock to another,

Six feet across,

A drop of one hundred feet separating the two large boulders,

My cousins ran back to my mother to brag about my daring,

My heroism.

But I didn't leap because I wanted to prove my mettle,

I leapt because I had to,

Because nature's beauty makes demands on us that we cannot refuse,

And because that leap brought me to a site where I could lie on my back

     Underneath the waterfall

And watch the play of light shimmer through the rushing water

     Like a dancing ghost who knows that she is being watched,

Like the spirit of a prophet who has returned because he knows the time is right.

KURT VONNEGUT

2 B R 0 2 B

Everything was perfectly swell.

There were no prisons, no slums, no insane asylums, no cripples, no poverty, no wars.

All diseases were conquered. So was old age.

Death, barring accidents, was an adventure for volunteers.

The population of the United States was stabilized at forty million souls.

One bright morning in the Chicago Lying-in Hospital, a man named Edward K. Wehling, Jr., waited for his wife to give birth. He was the only man waiting. Not many people were born a day any more.

Wehling was fifty-six, a mere stripling in a population whose average age was one hundred and twenty-nine.

X-rays had revealed that his wife was going to have triplets. The children would be his first.

Young Wehling was hunched in his chair, his head in his hand. He was so rumpled, so still and colorless as to be virtually invisible. His camouflage was perfect, since the waiting room had a disorderly and demoralized air, too. Chairs and ashtrays had been moved away from the walls. The floor was paved with spattered drop cloths.

The room was being redecorated. It was being redecorated as a memorial to a man who had volunteered to die.

A sardonic old man, about two hundred years old, sat on a stepladder, painting a mural he did not like. Back in the days when people aged visibly, his age would have been guessed at thirty-five or so. Aging had touched him that much before the cure for aging was found.

The mural he was working on depicted a very neat garden. Men and women in white, doctors and nurses, turned the soil, planted seedlings, sprayed bugs, spread fertilizer.

Men and women in purple uniforms pulled up weeds, cut down plants that were old and sickly, raked leaves, carried refuse to trash-burners.

Never, never, never—not even in medieval Holland nor old Japan— had a garden been more formal, been better tended. Every plant had all the loam, light, water, air and nourishment it could use.

A hospital orderly came down the corridor, singing under his breath a popular song:

> *If you don't like my kisses, honey,*
> *Here's what I will do:*
> *I'll go see a girl in purple,*
> *Kiss this sad world toodle-oo.*
> *If you don't want my lovin',*
> *Why should I take up all this space?*
> *I'll get off this old planet,*
> *Let some sweet baby have my place.*

The orderly looked in at the mural and the muralist. "Looks so real," he said, "I can practically imagine I'm standing in the middle of it."

"What makes you think you're not in it?" said the painter. He gave a satiric smile. "It's called 'The Happy Garden of Life,' you know."

"That's good of Dr. Hitz," said the orderly.

He was referring to one of the male figures in white, whose head was a portrait of Dr. Benjamin Hitz, the hospital's Chief Obstetrician. Hitz was a blindingly handsome man.

"Lot of faces still to fill in," said the orderly. He meant that the faces of many of the figures in the mural were still blank. All blanks were to be filled with portraits of important people on either the hospital staff or from the Chicago Office of the Federal Bureau of Termination.

"Must be nice to be able to make pictures that look like something," said the orderly.

The painter's face curdled with scorn. "You think I'm proud of this daub?" he said. "You think this is my idea of what life really looks like?"

"What's your idea of what life looks like?" said the orderly.

The painter gestured at a foul drop cloth. "There's a good picture of it," he said. "Frame that, and you'll have a picture a damn sight more honest than this one."

"You're a gloomy old duck, aren't you?" said the orderly.

"Is that a crime?" said the painter.

The orderly shrugged. "If you don't like it here, Grandpa—" he said, and he finished the thought with the trick telephone number that people who didn't want to live any more were supposed to call. The zero in the telephone number he pronounced "naught." The number was: "2 B R 0 2 B."

It was the telephone number of an institution whose fanciful sobriquets included: "Automat," "Birdland," "Cannery," "Catbox," "Delouser," "Easy-go," "Good-by, Mother," "Happy Hooligan," "Kiss-me-quick," "Lucky Pierre," "Sheepdip," "Waring Blendor," "Weep-no-more" and "Why Worry?"

"To be or not to be" was the telephone number of the municipal gas chambers of the Federal Bureau of Termination.

The painter thumbed his nose at the orderly. "When I decide it's time to go," he said, "it won't be at the Sheepdip."

"A do-it-yourselfer, eh?" said the orderly. "Messy business, Grandpa. Why don't you have a little consideration for the people who have to clean up after you?"

The painter expressed with an obscenity his lack of concern for the tribulations of his survivors. "The world could do with a good deal more mess, if you ask me," he said.

The orderly laughed and moved on.

Wehling, the waiting father, mumbled something without raising his head.

And then he fell silent again.

A coarse, formidable woman strode into the waiting room on spike heels. Her shoes, stockings, trench coat, bag and overseas cap were all purple, the purple the painter called "the color of grapes on Judgment Day."

The medallion on her purple musette bag was the seal of the Service Division of the Federal Bureau of Termination, an eagle perched on a turnstile.

The woman had a lot of facial hair—an unmistakable mustache, in fact. A curious thing about gas-chamber hostesses was that, no matter how lovely and feminine they were when recruited, they all sprouted mustaches within five years or so.

"Is this where I'm supposed to come?" she said to the painter.

"A lot would depend on what your business was," he said. "You aren't about to have a baby, are you?"

"They told me I was supposed to pose for some picture," she said. "My name's Leora Duncan." She waited.

"And you dunk people," he said.

"What?" she said.

"Skip it," he said.

"That sure is a beautiful picture," she said. "Looks just like heaven or something."

"Or something," said the painter. He took a list of names from his smock pocket. "Duncan, Duncan, Duncan," he said, scanning the list. "Yes—here you are. You're entitled to be immortalized. See any face-less body here you'd like me to stick your head on? We've got a few choice ones left."

She studied the mural bleakly. "Gee," she said, "they're all the same to me. I don't know anything about art."

"A body's a body, eh?" he said, "All righty. As a master of fine art, I recommend this body here." He indicated a faceless figure of a woman who was carrying dried stalks to a trash burner.

"Well," said Leora Duncan, "that's more the disposal people, isn't it? I mean, I'm in service. I don't do any disposing."

The painter clapped his hands in mock delight. "You say you don't know anything about art, and then you prove in the next breath that you know more about it than I do! Of course the sheave-carrier is wrong for a hostess! A snipper, a pruner—that's more your line." He pointed to a figure in purple who was sawing a dead branch from an apple tree. "How about her?" he said. "You like her at all?"

"Gosh—" she said, and she blushed and became humble— "that—that puts me right next to Dr. Hitz."

"That upsets you?" he said.

"Good gravy, no!" she said. "It's—it's just such an honor."

"Ah, You admire him, eh?" he said.

"Who doesn't admire him?" she said, worshiping the portrait of Hitz. It was the portrait of a tanned, white-haired, omnipotent Zeus, two hundred and forty years old. "Who doesn't admire him?" she said again. "He was responsible for setting up the very first gas chamber in Chicago."

"Nothing would please me more," said the painter, "than to put you next to him for all time. Sawing off a limb—that strikes you as appropriate?"

"That is kind of like what I do," she said. She was demure about what she did. What she did was make people comfortable while she killed them.

And, while Leora Duncan was posing for her portrait, into the waiting room bounded Dr. Hitz himself. He was seven feet tall, and he boomed with importance, accomplishments, and the joy of living.

"Well, Miss Duncan! Miss Duncan!" he said, and he made a joke. "What are you doing here?" he said. "This isn't where the people leave. This is where they come in!"

"We're going to be in the same picture together," she said shyly.

"Good!" said Dr. Hitz heartily. "And, say, isn't that some picture?"

"I sure am honored to be in it with you," she said.

"Let me tell you," he said, "I'm honored to be in it with you. Without women like you, this wonderful world we've got wouldn't be possible."

He saluted her and moved toward the door that led to the delivery rooms.

"Guess what was just born," he said.

"I can't," she said.

"Triplets!" he said.

"Triplets!" she said. She was exclaiming over the legal implications of triplets.

The law said that no newborn child could survive unless the parents of the child could find someone who would volunteer to die. Triplets, if they were all to live, called for three volunteers.

"Do the parents have three volunteers?" said Leora Duncan.

"Last I heard," said Dr. Hitz, "they had one, and were trying to scrape another two up."

"I don't think they made it," she said. "Nobody made three appointments with us. Nothing but singles going through today, unless somebody called in after I left. What's the name?"

"Wehling," said the waiting father, sitting up, red-eyed and frowzy.

"Edward K. Wehling, Jr., is the name of the happy father-to-be."

He raised his right hand, looked at a spot on the wall, gave a hoarsely wretched chuckle. "Present," he said.

"Oh, Mr. Wehling," said Dr. Hitz, "I didn't see you."

"The invisible man," said Wehling.

"They just phoned me that your triplets have been born," said Dr. Hitz. "They're all fine, and so is the mother. I'm on my way in to see them now."

"Hooray," said Wehling emptily.

"You don't sound very happy," said Dr. Hitz.

"What man in my shoes wouldn't be happy?" said Wehling. He gestured with his hands to symbolize carefree simplicity. "All I have to do is pick out which one of the triplets is going to live, then deliver my maternal grandfather to the Happy Hooligan, and come back here with a receipt."

Dr. Hitz became rather severe with Wehling, towered over him. "You don't believe in population control, Mr. Wehling?" he said.

"I think it's perfectly keen," said Wehling tautly.

"Would you like to go back to the good old days, when the population of the Earth was twenty billion—about to become forty billion, then eighty billion, then one hundred and sixty billion? Do you know what a drupelet is, Mr. Wehling?" said Hitz.

"Nope," said Wehling sulkily.

"A drupelet, Mr. Wehling, is one of the little knobs, one of the little pulpy grains of a blackberry," said Dr. Hitz. "Without population control, human beings would now be packed on this surface of this old planet like drupelets on a blackberry! Think of it!"

Wehling continued to stare at the same spot on the wall.

"In the year 2000," said Dr. Hitz, "before scientists stepped in and laid down the law, there wasn't even enough drinking water to go around, and nothing to eat but seaweed—and still people insisted on their right to reproduce like jackrabbits. And their right, if possible, to live forever."

"I want those kids," said Wehling quietly. "I want all three of them."

"Of course you do," said Dr. Hitz. "That's only human."

"I don't want my grandfather to die, either," said Wehling.

"Nobody's really happy about taking a close relative to the Catbox," said Dr. Hitz gently, sympathetically.

"I wish people wouldn't call it that," said Leora Duncan.

"What?" said Dr. Hitz.

"I wish people wouldn't call it 'the Catbox,' and things like that," she said. "It gives people the wrong impression."

"You're absolutely right," said Dr. Hitz. "Forgive me." He corrected himself, gave the municipal gas chambers their official title, a title no one ever used in conversation. "I should have said, 'Ethical Suicide Studios,'" he said.

"That sounds so much better," said Leora Duncan.

"This child of yours—whichever one you decide to keep, Mr. Wehling," said Dr. Hitz. "He or she is going to live on a happy, roomy, clean, rich planet, thanks to population control. In a garden like that mural there." He shook his head. "Two centuries ago, when I was a young man, it was a hell that nobody thought could last another twenty years. Now centuries of peace and plenty stretch before us as far as the imagination cares to travel."

He smiled luminously.

The smile faded as he saw that Wehling had just drawn a revolver.

Wehling shot Dr. Hitz dead. "There's room for one—a great big one," he said.

And then he shot Leora Duncan. "It's only death," he said to her as she fell. "There! Room for two."

And then he shot himself, making room for all three of his children.

Nobody came running. Nobody, seemingly, heard the shots.

The painter sat on the top of his stepladder, looking down reflectively on the sorry scene.

The painter pondered the mournful puzzle of life demanding to be born and, once born, demanding to be fruitful…to multiply and to live as long as possible—to do all that on a very small planet that would have to last forever.

All the answers that the painter could think of were grim. Even grimmer, surely, than a Catbox, a Happy Hooligan, an Easy Go. He thought of war.

He thought of plague. He thought of starvation.

He knew that he would never paint again. He let his paintbrush fall to the drop cloths below. And then he decided he had had about enough of life in the Happy Garden of Life, too, and he came slowly down from the ladder.

He took Wehling's pistol, really intending to shoot himself.

But he didn't have the nerve.

And then he saw the telephone booth in the corner of the room. He went to it, dialed the well-remembered number: "2 B R 0 2 B."

"Federal Bureau of Termination," said the very warm voice of a hostess.

"How soon could I get an appointment?" he asked, speaking very carefully.

"We could probably fit you in late this afternoon, sir," she said. "It might even be earlier, if we get a cancellation."

"All right," said the painter, "fit me in, if you please." And he gave her his name, spelling it out.

"Thank you, sir," said the hostess. "Your city thanks you; your country thanks you; your planet thanks you. But the deepest thanks of all is from future generations."

(Originally published in *Worlds of If,* January 1962)

ZACK HUNTER

WE ARE THE ONLY THINGS
THAT STAND IN THE WAY

After the harvest
  has been processed
and winter comes
  to etch in the new cycle
I stomp a trudge
  of mycelium indications
and breathe the dank ions
  of the steelhead upstream.
Little black cilia
  of Xanthoparmelia
reaching out from underneath
  toward the light.
Focus
  for now
is the time.
  Forever.
What can you do
  with this dwindling bloom
of moment?
  An endless warmth
of love nurturing growth
  is rooting along the surface
of the slide
examined by the scope.

ZACK HUNTER

HYPOGYMNIA PHYSODES

I had never before seen anything like it. Still to this day, even with the numerous attempts at replication, nothing has ever come close. I suppose that's just the way this all works, and I was foolish to think otherwise- but how else would I have learned that? You get once in a lifetime hints as if some kind of glitch or joke and can either listen and follow them deeper into the possibilities while laughing or just shrug them off and bury them as byproducts of reality. The choice is yours just as much as it isn't.

Some call this a game. A game where you play it, or it plays you, and it goes both ways simultaneously. Like a guitarist and his audience metabolizing psilocin and dancing to the solar rhythms zapping out of his fingers. Statues come alive to mirror. Their liquid glass ghosts illuminate the dark background radiation in motion. The intersecting waves of choice and flow cast ripples illusively through the window. There's only so much you can control in that spacesuit rental of yours as it accumulates its scars; the tattooed reminders of our own ancestor.

I'm playing with a puzzle of a broken mirror.

I still remember when I was coming to and could see absolutely nothing. There was nothing more I wanted than to see. All that laid before me was the mystery.

Piece by piece. Night by day. I find the ones that fit.

Although it may not be whole, or just seem like a reflection, it's pieced together enough now that I can at least see through the shattered cracks. It's not something that could ever be completed, but I'm about halfway there.

It presented itself as a passage. A channel that can shade the severity of time through its serpentine wisteria-laced maze. It oscillates and overlays everything like a static in the dark. Literally pulsates, or envelopes each other in a steady rhythm. Indigo and the opposite. Over and over and always. Gone like a trichocereus and a tumbleweed. Consumed like the kudzu where I found a praying mantis that took flight to my hand.

I looked closely at the ancient creature. It was looking up at me with its wings outstretched and holding a tiny piece of Hypogymnia physodes in its mouth. When it took off and flew away it left the small specimen of lichen in my hand. I knew from reading Dr. Shulgins notes exactly what this was and proceeded to harvest the abundance that surrounded me.

About twenty grams of olivetol was extracted and isolated via thin layer chromatography from a kilogram of dried material in my kitchen overlooking the dunes. Pandit Shivkumar Sharma was crystallizing the space as loud as my system would go. I then synthesized the terpenoid into tetrahydrocannabinolic acid using limonene and phosphoryl chloride. I ate thirty-three milligrams that night.

The night I first drank the light.

MERRILL FARNSWORTH

JUST ENOUGH POISON

I happened upon three rattlesnakes sunning on a rock under the West Texas sky. The dusty bolder was one of many jagged shapes dotting the parched landscape outside the gates of place called Camp Meeting. Those snakes are with me to this day.

In my eleventh year a blue Pontiac station wagon belonging to my family rolled into an enclave of cowboys. My father parked our new car between two dusty pickup trucks. We were guests of my maternal relatives, cattle ranchers who were deeply religious but too far-flung across the vast acreage of Texas to gather for weekly worship. They'd counted up the hours required to remain on the right side of an angry God and decided that four church services each day for five days straight would do the trick.

My Great Grandfather Tidwell and other ranchers scoured the hills on horseback for a place of worship. They found a grove of cedars and set up camp. Eventually simple cabins were constructed for each family. Wives and daughters sewed gingham curtains to hang across open-air windows. Camp Meeting went from ghost town to hallowed ground each August, a month too hot to wrangle, brand, or slaughter

During my visit, meals were served three times daily in one of the four family food sheds. Each structure featured a hand-painted sign bearing a surname that connected webs of aunts, uncles, and cousins, all sprung from the loins of proud patriarchs. By the time I sat down for a meal, generations of God-fearing relatives had been meeting each summer since 1902. My city-slicker family (even the smallest town in which each person was not somehow related to another was called a city) took meals with my mother's extended family. This is where I tasted my first cup of coffee—bitter and black. There was a big guffaw when I asked, using my best manners, for hot chocolate. My mother, a former calf roper, ordered me to drink my coffee. I did as I was told.

When my rancher relatives weren't eating or sleeping, they were sitting straight-backed and expressionless in the Tabernacle, a wooden structure with a hot tin roof. A pulpit fashioned from cottonwood marked the spot where various preachers took turns dispensing fire and brimstone. Women young and old, hair pinned up and wearing modest cotton dresses, fanned themselves with paper plates. Their menfolk wore their best cowboy boots and starched shirts patched with rings of salty sweat. My father wore a golf shirt, dress slacks, and wingtips.

This father of mine, a good-natured "city slicker" sat in the back row of the Tabernacle with a flask of whiskey hidden in his pocket, the perfect antidote for the biting rhetoric of sin and salvation. He had no use for the hocus pocus of religion. Soon enough he'd gather his wife and daughter and drive us out the gates back to our modern life. It was my Great Grandmother Tidwell who had summoned us here. She insisted that I, her only great granddaughter, be initiated into the ways of the cedar grove *in order to survive the wicked world*. My mother, still terrified of Granny Tidwell, did as she was told. My father was courteous to the old lady and she seemed to like him just fine.

Granny Tidwell, a widow, was a handsome white-haired, leather-faced woman who'd recently flown to Egypt to ride camels and explore pyramids. Kinfolk who'd never set foot out of Texas (by choice) gave her a hard time about these foreign adventures. She didn't care what they, or anyone else, thought about anything.

Her high chiseled cheekbones, hazel eyes, and beak-like nose gave her the appearance of a hawk. She seemed to have taken an interest in me and often looked my way as I sat at the back of the Tabernacle. I felt like a helpless rabbit trapped under her unnerving gaze and kept stone still, feeling as if I were missing every other breath. Years later, this woman would announce to flustered relatives she'd rather die than be trapped in an old folks home. She cut them out of her will and proved the victor when she died a few days later. It's clear the woman had powers.

Back to the snakes. A few mischief-prone "second cousins twice removed" took pity on me the third day of church-sitting and sent a signal to sneak with them out the back door of the Tabernacle. I felt Granny Tidwell's eyes on me and froze, my eyes locked on hers. She nodded, as if willing me to join my wayward cousins. I obeyed her. We fled into the hills like outlaws and a few minutes later I scrambled up onto a rock where I came face to face with the trio of rattlers. They didn't coil up, shake their rattles, or dart their tongues. The serpents simply lifted their heads and glared at me, annoyance flickering in their poison-green eyes. I was paralyzed with terror. They slithered away, possibly hissing and cursing.

My rowdy cousins found me standing still as a statue and delivered me back to the cedar grove, making me swear not tell anyone about the snakes lest they be forbidden to roam the hills. I was the only child to get a spanking for sneaking out of church. I didn't dare tell my mother that Granny Tidwell had sanctioned my journey into the hills or about my encounter with the rattlers.

Though the sun-soaked snakes didn't strike, a poisonous glare entered into me that day. That dose of venom killed off the scared rabbit inside my good little girl body. I feel those Texas rattlers rising in me at night as I walk alone through the streets of New York, Chicago, Kampala, and Nairobi. The instinctive glare within my blue eyes has not once paralyzed a person with terror but there's just enough poison to keep me safe in this wicked world.

PART IV

DARK GREEN

CLIFTON SNIDER

MIRACLE

The psyche changes:
fractured matter,
gray-green
         a stump
knocked off
clean
         in soil
moist & fed
daily:
         a shoot
punctures the dirt,
appears virgin,
the air, room,
the same,
         the psyche
recovered, returned
bone-ready.

       —from *Moonman: New and Selected Poems*
       (World Parade Books, 2012)

Dan Fante

LOST IN RAVENNA

If your lover is a dog—love dogs
If your heart is in the sea—love the sea
If your feet are on the sand of the desert—love the desert.
But nothing is to be gained here on my broken
TV set without life's gift of uncertainty
No peace
No ongoing love
No self-contained paradise
Can or will be mine until I appreciate my
Own lost-ness
Perhaps, then, I am Dante—or Caligula
But who I am is not what I consider myself to be
I am a being within a being—a heart beating with a
Heart—a whisper contained within a scream
I am the tiles on your church floor
And the shit on your streets
I am my greatest friend & my most hated enemy
I am part of history & the hope of the future
I am the man next to you on the train
Or your most feared executioner
I am my own best friend in a world of
Orchestrated chaos
In fact—I am a piece of eternity
I am who I say I am
Strangely, my experience is that man
Is most perfect
When he believes himself to be lost.

"The great advantage of being a writer is that you can spy on people. You're there, listening to every word, but part of you is observing. Everything is useful to a writer, you see—every scrap, even the longest and most boring of luncheon parties.

GRAHAM GREENE

DONNA HILBERT

SEATTLE

" . . . but Wilson had no car. He felt almost intolerably lonely."

Graham Greene, *The Heart of the Matter*

So homesick, I engaged wrong numbers
in conversation
for the sound of another
human voice
that year in Seattle when it rained three hundred days.
Not hard as it would at home
and then be done for months,
but just a light piss,
air always damp
like the baby's diaper.
I watched pink fingers of mold
double every day
in the corner of the window
looking out on evergreens and endless grass.
I longed for LA—
palm trees and Hybrid Bermuda,
trees that let in light and grass with grace
enough to die back
yellow in the winter.
I hated the rain the natives praised
"rain makes everything green," they'd say,
deranged as they were on chlorophyll and caffeine.
I was green too at nineteen,
with a shiny new husband, one baby,
belly ripening with the next.
My husband studied engineering at the U.
And I studied too—his books from World Lit—
Dostoevsky, Kafka, Camus.
My favorite was Graham Greene
The Power and the Glory, The Heart of the Matter—
burnt-out-cases
adrift in the existential sea.
And I thought then that I
was more displaced
than any whiskey priest or disaffected spy
which I declared to any wrong number
who would take the time
to listen.

MORIAH LaCHAPELL

GREEN

felt board Sunday school stories
Isaac's redemption
came from a Ram
Lot's wife became salt
because she looked back
righteous anger
in the smell
of graham crackers
peanut butter and itchy tights
stand in line
recite the story
get a piece of candy
God will provide.

DICTATION

listen
to the voice
wrap yourself in words
like silken green sheets
(know you are
still beautiful)
forget reality
for a little while
at least.

Jax NTP

neurosity lxxxviii

in memory of my emotions

my anxiety has a baby rattlesnake in it, the babes are most dangerous
because they've yet to learn how to control their venom—my anxiety
has a number of naked selves, the accumulation of conversations

that i've excluded or have been excluded from, the poetics of negation,
when women are stressed, especially during wartime, the production
of cortisone decreases and they are more likely to give birth to girls,

the correlation between tree density and population density per square
mile, how the wealthy plant more trees, aesthetically pleasing, spiritually
uplifting, the way we make the same decisions over and over and over

and over again, the price of being poor, transformations of the self,
salmon roulettes and crudités, loss of hearing, mechanical cranes,
to be deaf, but not deft-less, the biscuits and gravy of poetry,

text messages are the fragments of communication engineered
by modern technology, the arrangements of physical bodies, the different
implications of what it means to sit next to versus across from—my anxiety

renovates the womb, my anxiety renovates the womb, one fact at a time,
the ability to create forms, the quiet world of phosphenes, the nebulous
galaxies you see when you rub your eyes, the maple seduction of pearl

everlastings, not sunset green, but sinatra blue, not sunset green,
but sinatra blue, the way we suffer more from imagination than reality,
a meditative space between pages, paper cities and weights on clavicles,

the dictionary's synonyms for coincidence: accident, luck, and/or fate,
the ability to render nothingness into the state of fullness, there is no
such thing as a non-habit-forming sleep aid, there is no such thing

as a non-habit-forming sleep aid, well, good morning midnight

Jax NTP

my dear lorca,

the starchy quietness of my room is louder than the anatomy of the night.
since i came back from paris, the land outside my window is still dry. if
it were not for the hymns of my shyness, the fulcrum of our swords would cross.

pain is the architecture of loneliness and the small conversations i have with myself.
what constitutes denial is gathered up in cloves of phantom ships. if it were not
for the stories of my shyness, gala would have never been my wife. the persistence
of my memory reveals the hidden corals and conches i paint for you.

but even my subconscious is not patient enough for your poetry.
the olive wind whispers your name in sierra. and i hate that it haunts
me. tonight, the catalan lights shine on the binary breasts of roses.
and still, i live in the penumbra of your absence.

always,
salvador dali

Jax NTP

why i am not a prose writer
a personal defense of poetry

because there is no money
and there are no adventures
in a poem and that is familiar
and familiarity comforts me

because who needs a fireplace
in winter when the sizzles
of dying leaves beget birth

because linear prose is constant chatter
and continuity makes me anxious,
but glorified bar talk from bukowski
and the waste land are enough to keep
me excited without being too attached

because writing prose is like smoking
with a lighter but poems are like matches,
the sulfur dioxide, reminds me of a girl
i once loved, the texture of her hair at bonfires

because the politics of prepositions tyrannize
lengths of loss and sharp corners of grief
where pupils are hourglasses filled with ashes

because i indulge in the rush,
mastered the art of rushing
to get there and manically
rushing to get away

because before "morning dew"
turned into a post-apocalyptic
folk song, it was a poem

ELLARAINE LOCKIE

AUTOPSY MEANS TO SEE WITH ONE'S OWN EYES

In death she relaxes, parts her legs willingly
Watches with a spirit's fly eyes
the white gowns hovering over her
Hands holding, knives, chisels, scalpels and saws
in a room bleached of color

> *He bent over her*
> *weight feeding through one leg onto her belly*
> *The blade flashed an echo of car light into the alley*
> *A siren slashed the night*
> *Too distant to be a soldier's song*

The first cut forms a Y from shoulders
to sternum to her pubic bone
Rivers of blood flow into a steel gutter at table's edge
Somewhere Chopin plays a nocturne

> *She smelled the blood before she felt its*
> *hydrant flood from the ear-to-ear smile on her throat*
> *Smooth and welcomed after the rage of storm*
> *Then the red gargle*

Curvature of stomach is cut and emptied
Intestines drained in a sink
The easy way to excrete
Even the stink lounges on impervious air
Behind masks come murmurs
about police awaiting what she had for dinner

> *Her spirit eyes didn't blink when a rat*
> *ran over her face or later when cameras flashed*
> *Red pools rusted thick and sticky*
> *Dispatch radios scratched the surface of sound*

Debris of Bordeaux, mesclun, escargot and green
peppercorns place her at the Encore Bistro Francais
from nine to midnight

> *She still sees the red wine, blood of Christ*
> *gracefully drip from the bottle onto white linen*

ELLARAINE LOCKIE

DR. HAUSER

I walk my college campus
recounting decades-old conversations
Close auditory connections between a co-ed
as green as grass before frost
and her middle-aged advisor

His words hang heavy
Ripe with interest beyond intellectual
Logic displayed only in his Ph.D.
philosophy diploma

His implied intimacy unrecognized
Naiveté blinding me
to ascot sophistication
sensuous drags on a dry pipe
and longing in dark brown eyes
His look lost to sororities, Beatles music
and football player physiques

I'd know the look now though
Recognize it in regions below eyes
I'd hear the silent hunger
His look now lost to adult diapers
defective hearing aid
and stories told too many times
The green seasoned to grey

ELLARAINE LOCKIE

IRONY AT THE ALLERGIST'S

Plastic replaces bona fide flowers and pollen
on the table by a stack of magazines
You think you can smell neroli
from the bittersweet blossoms
on the cover of *The Green Gardener*
Or maybe it's the gray cat curled
around the tree trunk that's causing
your nose to raise its voice

First the whine of sniffles sends you
to the box of Kleenex on the corner table
Then the blast in a trombone's decibel range
that causes a woman to drop her pill
Followed by a continued ensemble of sneezes
as Georgia O'Keeffe's purple petunias
on the wall waft optic allergens
And oak branches outside brush their own
allergy onslaught against the skylight

You know by feel that the flowers
beside the Kleenex are silk
Yet your eyes want to water them
Someone offers a Benedryl
but you can't accept the absurdity
You feel even more foolish to find
from the allergist that dust and molds
are your real antagonists

With 179 needle scratches that leave
back and arms with enough red welts
to evoke a battered woman
You return *Better Homes and Gardens*
to the waiting room table
Brush against a plastic sunflower branch
And gray powders storm the air
that the biggest welt on your arm
welcomes like long-lost relatives

DALE SPROWL

LADY, TIGER AND TLC

I'm a lab rat,
caged, crazed, raged.

I tongue a metal water spout
and eat pressed green pellets,
mmm.

I even have my own treadmill,
to stay healthy and relieve stress,
of course.

At night, I crawl under a blanket of warm wood shavings
and dream my freedom dreams.
Sometimes, though, I dream about drowning,
or falling off the laboratory table;
sometimes I dream of checkerboards
or the air swarming with flies.

Each day is the same.
I'm picked up by a human hand
and placed inside a maze.

The maze is different everyday.
Sometimes I run through it and get tiny electrical shocks;
Sometimes I get pellets,
but I never get out.

There are two doors that lead out of the maze.
One is sealed shut. It has a "T" on it.
Even if I reach it, I cannot exit there.
When I find it, I hold my nose high,
close my black rat eyeballs and breathe deeply. Thrice.
I sniff all around the edges.
I like the scent of the unopenable door.

Since I can't go that way, I run around some more,
looking for the exit. The one marked "L".
I haven't found it yet.

Some days before I run the maze, the human hand
gives me a shot of adrenaline.
Other days a finger forces me to swallow a pill that slows me down.

➤

Then I scurry either faster or slower
searching for open passageways, ways to proceed.
Maybe, maybe if I could gather all my strength,
I could push up on the glass ceiling above me and squeeze out.
Or maybe, if I were smart and the human hand lazy,
I could roll myself into a ball and hide in the corner.
Then at night, when no one's looking,
I could scratch and scrape and gnaw and burrow out.
Maybe I could throw myself against a wall of the mad rat labyrinth
and it would fall and I could skulk away.

Maybe I'll just keep pushing and running,
rolling and hiding,
scratching and burrowing.
Or maybe I'll find the door,
the freedom dream door.

What is it like beyond that door?
I can only guess.
The "L," what does it mean?
Maybe if I become an "L,"
I'll be able to go around the outside of the box,
find the door marked "T" and open it from the outside.
Maybe when I'm a real "L," I'll be able to be a real "T" too.
A novel idea for a rat.

Maybe I won't feel like I have to do anything.
Maybe I'll think here and now is all there is.
Maybe I'll think there's more, and I can get what I want,
that I can have it all.
Maybe when I dream outside the door,
I won't dream of checkerboards and drowning, falling and flies.
Maybe I will.

Maybe I'll do what I feel like and like what I feel.
Maybe I'll want what I have and have what I want.
Maybe I'll wonder what the human hand is doing and
what is happening in the maze.
I think I'll miss it.
There's something about it that I like.
Maybe I'll sneak back at night and explore it,
or maybe it will be inside me, my own creation,
a complicated maze with lots of open doors, no glass atop,
and one without walls of separation.

I wonder, a rat has to wonder, about what is beyond that door.

MELANIE VILLINES

GREEN FLUORESCENT GLOW

Vance Middlebrooks's stomach growled as he groped in the darkness toward the line of light. He had skipped breakfast and lunch, and now his body was roaring for food. He felt lightheaded as he reached out and moved his hands across what he hoped was a door, until he felt a doorknob. He grabbed onto the knob, turned it, and pulled, then eased the door open enough so he could see through a slit on the side.

He saw a room lit with a green florescent glow, then cracked the door a bit more and saw people sitting on folding chairs. They all had their eyes closed and seemed to be either asleep or meditating.

Vance had had enough of this crazy job, where nobody would tell him what he was supposed to do. He needed to get out, needed to go home—and, most of all, he needed to eat.

Vance took a deep breath, flung open the door, then ran into the room, turning to his right and left looking for a way out. But there was no way out. It was a room with no windows and no doors other than the one he'd entered. He heard the door slam shut behind him.

"Well, I see you've found us," he heard Dr. Bing say.

Vance turned and saw the hulking, lumberjack-attired Dr. Bing standing dead center in circle of folding chairs. In the chairs was an assortment of men—about ten white, black, and brown (but no Asian) individuals—in ages ranging from late adolescence to early middle age. None of the men looked at Vance. They all sat staring at the floor with their hands folded in their laps.

"Have a seat, Maxwell," Vance heard Griffin Gnowles call out—addressing him by someone else's name, as he'd done when Vance had first arrived at what he thought was a writing gig. Vance still had no idea what was going on or why he had been called to the location.

Vance turned and saw the red-carpet interviewer emerge from behind a room divider, accompanied by a man holding a video camera, a man holding a spotlight, and another toting a microphone.

Vance made his way toward Griffin, and when he was close said in a low voice, "I need to leave. Let me out of here."

"You signed up for this gig," Griffin said.

"And what am I supposed to do?" Vance asked.

Griffin aimed his cold green stare into Vance's eyes.

"Isn't it obvious?"

"Not to me."

"I hired you for a writing gig," Griffin said. "You're here to gather information for a script."

With that, Griffin turned and strode into the circle of men and stood next to Dr. Bing, who addressed the gathering.

"Thank you for agreeing to participate in this valuable project. Today, none other than Griffin Gnowles, whom I'm sure you've seen many times on television, will interview you about your experiences with and feelings about taking Zronapine. It is our hope that others may be helped when they hear stories about how your lives have improved thanks to Zronapine."

As Vance listened to Dr. Bing, he tried to figure out if he should take notes. The only notebook he had with him was the one he'd just filled up with his screenplay notes when he'd ducked into a restroom a short time before, and he didn't want to take a chance at losing or leaving it behind, or, worse, having somebody steal it from him (was he getting paranoid?). He patted the pocket of his green parka to make sure the notebook was still there. Vance decided that he didn't need to take notes. After all, the video and audio people were picking up everything. He figured he'd get a transcript of all the pertinent information if they wanted him to write a script about the drug—whatever it was.

The next thing Vance knew, Bing was finishing his homey chat with the crowd. The doctor turned to the celebrity interviewer and said, "Griffin…"

Griffin clasped his hands together as if overcome with joy, then took a moment to give each man a brief glance—his way of bestowing a special blessing.

"Welcome!" Griffin boomed, then extended his hands to include one and all.

Vance couldn't believe Griffin was using his unctuous television personality in these circumstances. And "welcome"? Good God, these men lived here, didn't they?

"…we're so happy you've decided to join us today to share your thoughts about Zronapine. We are looking for…"

A small black man jumped up and yelled, "When do we get the twenty bucks?"

Dr. Bing rushed into the circle and from his great height put his huge hands on the man's shoulders and pushed him back into his chair.

"You know better than that, Dwight," Bing chided. "It was all explained to you earlier."

"Tell me again," Dwight said in a soft voice as he gazed up at Bing.

"You will be paid *after* your interview," Bing told him.

Griffin stepped in and said, "It's not really a payment. It's an honorarium. It's our way of showing appreciation for your time."

"What's the difference?" Dwight asked.

"That's enough," Bing said. "Now please hold your questions. You will be called on one by one. While one of you is being interviewed, I expect the rest of you to sit quietly and wait your turn."

The men started to shift in their chairs. Griffin picked up on their body language.

"Perhaps, Dr. Bing," Griffin said, "it would be advisable for the men to spend the interim in a recreational area. That way, they can watch television while they're waiting."

"If you prefer," Bing said.

"I do," Griffin replied.

With that, the men got up *en masse* and headed for the door. As they did, Bing called out to one of them.

"Barry, please stay," Bing told him. "You can be first."

Vance looked around for Barry. Before he spotted anyone, he heard a man shout out, "Why am I the first one?"

Vance assumed that Barry was the man now standing with his back against the wall next to the doorway. He was a guy in his early twenties of medium height with wavy shoulder-length blonde hair and a brownish beard—your basic surfer dude.

Dr. Bing strutted up to Barry, leaned down, and spoke about two inches from his face. "Because your story is so dramatic, Barry. The change in you has been amazing. All because of Zronapine."

Surfer Barry turned his eyes into slits and looked up at Bing, as if trying to protect his sight from harmful solar rays. He didn't say anything, but seemed to be thinking of a few choice words he wanted to spit out. After a moment, he shrugged and looked away from Bing.

"This way, Barry," Griffin said, indicating the area behind the room divider.

Barry pushed himself away from the wall and strolled toward Griffin. His whole body seemed to be rolling, as if he had extra joints from head to toe.

As Barry approached, Vance sat up straight in his chair. He was so hungry that he was starting to feel numb and dizzy.

Vance stood up and followed Barry to the area behind the room divider. It looked like an interrogation room. Griffin was seated behind a long folding table with the people operating the camera, audio equipment, and lights ready to roll. There was a folding chair at either end of the table.

"Barry, take this seat. Maxwell, take that seat.," Griffin instructed.

The two men complied.

Griffin straightened his Armani tie, squared his shoulders, took a long, deep breath, then exhaled. He put on his sunniest red-carpet smile, looked at Barry and said, "Before we start, let me talk a bit about why we're here today."

"Skip it," Barry said, scratching his beard. "I know why we're here."

"Well, please indulge me, Barry," Griffin said, the smile never leaving his face. "I have to adhere to protocol."

"You want to ask me about taking Zronapine," Barry told him. "What else do I need to know?"

"The drug manufacturer wants to make sure I explain things clearly before we proceed," Griffin explained. "We need to be certain that all of your comments are freely given."

Barry turned to Vance, pointed, and asked: "Who's he?"

"He's our writer," Griffin explained. "His name is Maxwell."

For once, Vance was glad that they hadn't used his real name.

"I don't see him writing," Barry said.

"Maxwell will write a script based on what he learns here today."

"A script for what?" Barry asked.

"I thought you understood," Griffin began, "that we're here to learn about your experiences taking Zronapine, and we may use that information in a script."

"Like I said," Barry hissed, "a script for what?"

"It's for an informed-consent video," Griffin said. "When a doctor prescribes Zronapine, a patient will watch the video to get information about the drug."

"So why do you need to know about me?" Barry said.

"Because it shows the personal side of the story, how the drug improves people's lives."

"People wouldn't have to watch a video like that," Barry said, "unless the drug had a lot of bad side effects."

From his spot on the sidelines, Vance realized that Barry had turned the tables on Griffin. He had assumed the role of the interviewer and was interrogating the professional question asker.

The smile evaporated from Griffin's face and he wore a pained look, as if his expensive Italian shoes were two sizes too small. Finally, he spoke.

"The video will explain the benefits of Zronapine as well as the potential side effects," Griffin said in a voice devoid of its usual chirpiness.

Barry's eyes shifted from side to side like the pendulum of a clock. He was thinking over what he'd just heard. After taking a few deep breaths, he turned his gaze to Griffin.

"What are you doing here?" Barry asked.

"I just explained…"

"No, I mean why *you*," Barry said. "Why is a TV guy doing a job like this?"

"I don't see how that's relevant," Griffin said.

"I just want to know," Barry told him.

"A friend of mine works for the pharmaceutical company," Griffin replied. "He asked me to do this as a favor to him."

Barry stood up and took a step toward Griffin, who leaned back in his chair.

"What do you know about schizophrenia or atypical antipsychotic drugs?" Barry said, glaring into Griffin's eyes.

Griffin sat up straight, then appeared to fold into himself, as if trying to disappear or hope that if he didn't move or didn't breathe, Barry would assume a friendly disposition.

"Huh?" Barry asked, jerking his head forward, his eyes blazing.

When Griffin didn't respond, Barry pounded on the table with both of his open palms.

"What gives you the right," Barry said, "to waltz in here and start asking about things you know nothing about? Do you think because you ask Grade-Z celebrities about their rat-ass clothes and fricking reality shows that you have the right to come in here and interview people with a chronic disease about their illness?"

As Barry continued to rant, Vance was enthralled. Finally, somebody was speaking some sense in a totally absurd situation—and Vance's entire life in LA. was filled with absurd situations that remained unaddressed.

"…you're nothing but a vampire and a pimp…" Barry said as he berated Griffin.

Griffin tilted his head toward Vance and whispered out of the corner of his mouth: "Go find Dr. Bing."

"…I want my twenty bucks, you mother…" Barry ranted.

Vance stood up and the whole room started spinning. He felt as if he were floating on a flimsy carpet that undulated around the room. He knew right away what was wrong. His blood sugar had finally gotten the best of him. He couldn't go on any longer without food. Vance wobbled on his feet, hitting his left temple on the table as he fell to the floor.

The last thing he remembered was the buzzing of the fluorescent light and the room spinning in a downward spiral like a glowing green whirlpool.

JACK MICHELINE

GRANT & GREEN

Keep your head high chappie
it's a cold night out there
there's Tommy the hook
his magician's hat and conjurer's trade

For lonely sailors
guys with dreams
long lost loves and adding machines

Keep the whiskey flowing
Keep the juice alive
keep your head high chappie
it's a cold night out there
Love is gone out the window
Let's go to fantasyland

Willy is there
Tony is there
Gino with his sad eyes and expressive hands

The jukebox is playing
the endless booze
all the girls look beautiful
liquid is flowing like a waterfall
the Indian girl Joie keeps walking through the door
the old guy on the bar stool
he's been there since '64

A round for everybody
the poor bloke says
he wants to go home
and paint on his wall
he's gone crazy on the endless street
where people too sensitive and lovers meet

The crazy Russian Jew Jack
with them wild crazy tales
of redheaded chicks
and girls in the slam
and vagabonds and Chicanos
tough guys and the blonds
➤

Keep it flowing chappie
on a merry-go-round
see that guy on the street
he took out his cock
and let flow a log leak
right on my floor
I'll kill that bastard someday
he's not coming in here no more

You're looking for a buddy
You know he's in the bar
He's got the same seat for years since 1964
So keep your head high buddy
there'll always be a war
and all the girls are beautiful
and the liquid flows like a waterfall

There's Specs with the old jokes
postcards from the working class
Jack Micheline
his museum on the wall
Bobby Miller jokes were classic in 1954
Bob Kaufman humming symphonies
Big Jim still dreaming looking for the girls
Foxy's laughing like a maniac
Gini he hit Keno $554
Bustop Whitey cleaned out Ruggles
right on Carlo's floor

Sam and John and Sally
Barbara, Alice, Blue
Big Jim, Gene and Jerry
Big Black, Red and Blue
The stage is always open
on the corner of Grant and Green
the hook standing there smiling
his big hat in his hand
keep your head high chappie
there'll always be a war

It's open house day and night
on the corner of Grant and Green
Willy is there
Tony is there
Gino the conductor
the Indian girl Joie she's walking through the door

and the tall guy on the bar stool
he's been there since '64
The liquid keeps flowing
just like a waterfall
it's a cruel world Buddy
it's an adding machine
it's a carousel
it's a merry-go-round
it's an open house in the afternoon
On the corner of Grant and Green

There's Russian Jack the madman
he's laughing on his flying machine
put the magicians on the airplane
put the conjurers against the wall
put the politicians in the madhouse
and the poets on the floor

And the Indian girl Joie
Keeps walking in the door
and that guy's still walking the street
for twenty years or more
and the tall guy on the bar stool
he's been here since '64

It's a cruel world Buddy
it's an adding machine
everything flows so easy
on the corner of Grant and Green
Foxy's laughing like a maniac

Russian Jack on his flying machine
put the magicians on an airplane
put the conjurers against the wall
put the politicians in a mad house
and the poets on the floor

Keep your head high chappie
there's a cold night out there
there's that guy on the bar stool
he's been here since '64
three feet from reality
three feet from the door
Keep your head high chappie
you're just three feet from the door.

Photo of Jack Micheline (1982) © by Eddie Woods.

JACK MICHELINE

AN INTERVIEW BY EDDIE WOODS

Eddie Woods interviewed poet Jack Micheline on December 7, 1982, three days after Micheline's reading at *Ins & Outs Press* (later released as a spoken-word audio cassette entitled *Jack Micheline in Amsterdam*).* Micheline had flown to Amsterdam, all expenses paid, to appear at the annual One World Poetry Festival and was staying as Eddie's guest in a top-floor apartment of the Ins & Outs building, next door to a seventeenth century church on the quiet fringe of the garishly bustling red-light district. It was a busy and rewarding year for Micheline—a few months earlier, he'd been voted "most valuable poet" at a Kerouac festival sponsored by Naropa Institute in Boulder, Colorado, an event he was able to attend because enthusiastic friends in San Francisco had raised his bus fare. He had also performed at the Poetry Olympics in London. Before returning to the U.S., he enjoyed a highly successful exhibition of his paintings at an Amsterdam gallery.

Eddie Woods and Jack Micheline again met in the Netherlands ten years later, when they performed together at the 1992 North Sea Jazz Festival. Although the two maintained a lively correspondence until shortly before Jack's death in February 1998, this interview was misplaced in the shuffle of vicissitudes and only recently resurfaced.

Note: For the **Silver Birch Press** *Green Anthology*, this interview has been condensed to about one-quarter of its original content. Read the entire interview at this link:

http://www.corpse.org/archives/issue_11/critiques/woods.html

---

* * *Jack Micheline in Amsterdam was* re-released in 2012 on CD by Unrequited Records (San Francisco).

EW: You said that you're not a professional poet.

JM: Hell, no. I've never been a professional poet in my life. I live it. I walk in the streets and I get the message and I write it down. What professional poet? I never graduated high school.

EW: So what is a professional poet?

JM: All right, a professional poet is somebody who hustles and makes a living from the shit, or who tries to make a living from it. And a living poet is every minute you are a poet, you don't have to write to be a poet. A shoemaker could be the greatest poet…So it isn't what you say, it's what you do that makes you a poet.

EW: But aren't there some, what you would call professional poets, who are also living poets?

JM: Right, sure, they study the poems, they read everybody else who comes out. They read in the universities. They get the rich people to back them or the big companies to publish them. But to me they are not saying anything. So they might have good use of language, they may write some interesting poems; but they are not moving it out to the masses, they are not saying anything to the people who are dead, who are the living dead. And the idea of a poet is to wake up the dead, shake up the ones who cannot think, cannot smell, taste, feel, or breathe. And so they are not revolutionaries in the sense of trying to shake up the system. They want a piece of the action and they want to be rich and famous and they do not want to shake up anything. They are not revolutionaries. They are not people who are willing to put their life on the line to change the system or to make the world a better place for most people to live in. In other words, they are doing it for the money.

EW: Are you saying that commercial or academic success is, of necessity, incompatible with being a real poet? So I repeat: are there no, what you call professional poets, who are nonetheless writing "living poetry"?

JM: They breathe and they let live and they work hard and they are craftsmen. They are good at their craft. But my poetry has nothing to do with anyone else writing today. It has got to do with my vision, which is very personal, very in tune with the whole universe, with what I consider to be the universe. I don't write for other poets and I don't write to be accepted by the academy. I don't even send my work to the academy.

EW: How about what the writing of a poem does for you?

JM: It's good when you write a poem you like. When I do a good painting I feel good, and it feels good when you write a good poem. That's the reward in itself. What comes afterwards is something else.

EW: I'm talking about the act of writing...

JM: The act of creation...

EW: Yes, when you make a discovery.

JM: I walk out in the night and I take one step and then another, right? Lorca spoke about duende, he talked about the spirit. He made a speech at Havana University in 1929. A young student said, "Mr. Lorca, could you tell us about the act of creation itself? What is the spirit that moves you?" And Lorca replied, "I do not write my poems, the spirit writes them for me. The duende writes the poems for me." And this is what he later said: "Most of these guys, the duende doesn't write for them. They're craftsmen. They know language, they know images. But it isn't the spirit that moves them. Only the blessed ones, the great ones, are blest with this gift, to open themselves up and let the spirit write."

EW: You wrote somewhere something like "not for me the polished line or the line that's rewritten."

JM: I don't rewrite. Most of my work I do not rewrite; very rarely, unless it's an obvious flaw or a bad line. But there are very few flaws because I write from a high source...

EW: There are those who say one should never rewrite. That you should pen everything spontaneously, put the words down as they come, and then leave them alone. Do you go with that?

JM: Hey, man, there's no two people alike. Everyone is different. I have what I consider is an affirmation. I use poetry as a crutch, as a club, as a stepping stone, as a cane to keep on walking, to affirm my life, my spirit. I use it to keep my spirit going...The poem is me and I am the poem. There's no separation between my life and my work, and that's important. There is no separation. I am the poem.

EW: Dylan Thomas lived poetry all his life, and was a great poet. And he rewrote his poems over and over again, up to a hundred times for one poem.

JM: He was a craftsman. God bless him, he had the strength and energy to do it. I came out of the street, I wrote on the street. I wrote my ballads, I never studied ballads. I learned to write the ballad by doing it. My worst subject in school was English. But I'm a freak. I'm a freak that comes out into poetry. It was a blessed event, it enriched my life. I never dreamt I'd be a poet, let alone have the capacity to create poetry.

EW: Let's get back to that question of what poetry's about.

JM: I like to communicate. Like one time in Bughouse Square in Chicago. I was kicked out of this rooming house. It was in the late fifties and it was a warm summer night and I sat down under a tree and began reading my poems. And within five minutes there was a group of working people around me and someone took off their hat and asked someone else to pass the hat. I raised sixty dollars from those people and that was from reciting my poems about the city of Chicago. That was a high moment in my life, that I could move these working people to dig into their pockets, because I blessed them and they blessed me back with the cash.

EW: ...Have you also had the experience of writing something that you knew was so good, so meaningful, so perfect in your own terms, that no matter what anyone else might ever think of it, you're happy with it?

JM: Of course! Hey, if never sent a poem out—and I very rarely do, only when someone asks me and I like the people—I would still get my payoff when I write a good poem. Now if it gets published, that's a bonus. But most poets want to get published as much as they can. I look at it as way of life. I paint for my child, my child feeling. My colors are my child. The writing is my seriousness...It saved my life, poetry, because where I came from was a gangster mentality...And so when I got out of a ditch, somewhere in Illinois, and started writing fragments, just fragments in the beginning, it was a new life.

EW: Is happiness, or the concept of happiness, in any way an important quality of feeling in your life?

JM: My life has been tragic, very tragic. Anyone born with any genius, who sees a direct light to things, relates to very few people. Kline, the painter, lived a tragic life, died at fifty-two; James T. Farrell, Jack Kerouac, Charlie Mingus...people who were close to me. Most of the people I've known have not led happy lives. Why? Because they're out there, they're out there trying to find new things and some people resent that. They're explorers of the mind, explorers of the senses, always moving out into new spaces, always looking for new mountains to climb. And when they fall off the mountain, it'll take maybe a year to get back on the track of climbing another mountain. So you are always retracing your steps. Come falling down, getting up, taking a blow. No one wants to see a genius live to be recognized because, you see, they shake up the dead...Very few geniuses survive. They usually die very young. I know this.

EW: Do you? Victor Hugo lived to eighty-three or something. Henry Miller went west a year or so ago at what, eighty-eight, eighty-nine? Da Vinci nearly made seventy, which wasn't exactly young for his time. You mention James Farrell and he was seventy-five, for chrissake! So c'mon.

JM: Okay, okay! I said "usually."

EW: You talk about moments…

JM: The only moments in life are when you can get above the normal state that most everybody is in and really rise up and do it. Do a good job, write a good poem, make a good painting. I paint a lot. I've done a lot of fine paintings. I've written many fine poems. And when I'm do-ing it, when I'm absorbed in the creative act, the very doing is the deed…When you write, you must write with total involvement, you must be utterly taken by the activity. Those moments are what you live for. And if you have many such moments in life, then you are rich, richer than most people. More than any of those greedy dudes with bags full of hundred dollar bills or thousand dollar bills or millionaires who can't even write their names properly, all they do is sign checks. Because they haven't got the spirit or the light. They don't know what the moment is. So they buy art all their lives and try in that way to cap-ture what the artist has created. But they'll never have it. Sad, these guys. Thousands of millionaires who don't know about beauty, truth, or the moment.

[Sings]
And you can't put a moment in bottle
And you can't put a moment in a can
You gotta take a walk in the sunshine
And do the best you can.
That just came off the top of my head.
[Sings again]
Sunny Jim in the morning
Sunny Jim at night

Gonna walk my head off, mama,
Until I get it right.
Comin' home, oh I'm comin' home,
With that ole train at five o'clock,
Comin' home, comin' home,
Gonna sing that song, comin' home.
I'm sitting with Eddie Woods
Here in Amsterdam,
He's got a funny smile on his face.
A dog named Snuffie's in the back,
He's got a smile on his face.
Comin' home, comin' home,
Oh, baby, I'm comin' hoooooome.

The moment, we've gotta find out what the moment's about. And then we got it, we got it. Maybe I'll have a purple shirt on in a year. And I'll climb down from a mountain. Now this I doubt this, but...the purple people walking all over America, competing with the orange people and the green people and the black people and the blue people. Who knows? It's a great time ahead. Your life is always exciting. Always new challenges, new mountains. You never know what's going to happen. Good times are coming, America...The time is now, the time is ripe. Coming home, coming home, oh baby I'm coming hooooooome...!

The full text of this interview was originally published in *Exquisite Corpse* (online issue #11, Spring 2002) and reappeared in *Beat Scene* (issue #63, Winter 2010).

EDDIE WOODS

CLEAR QUEER GREEN

Clear queer green on metal white
Flowers blooming out of sight
Breaking light through mists of dawn
Petals open to the lawn

Dim and foreign figures wrought
Where sunny starmates come to naught
Tangled dreams on brittle dew
As thoughts seep down beyond our view

O stay, she cried to the dragon wild
Who clutched and bellowed at her child
But the monster fled with a sudden tear
That belched in flames o'er the golden bier

Aiee, serpents brewing in the trees of Spain
Cast scarlet shadows on the horse's mane
Then the stallion mingled his fear with fright
And charged in glory through the homespun night

Come tell me your troubles
My ancient brothers
Or my geese may never come home

I'll tell you, they sighed
As they lay down and died
In the twinkle of an old orange moon.

COLLEEN DELEGAN

IT'S ONLY A MATTER OF TIME

NOVEL EXCERPT

CHAPTER ONE

In her dream last night, she was kissing a lovely man. It wasn't the kiss that was so important, but rather the feeling that this person really cared for her, in fact, loved her. Then he suggested they go up to the apartment on the fifth floor, that this apartment could be theirs. She was ecstatic.

"Really? The fifth floor?" she said. "The views will be terrific."

He took her hand, and they rode the elevator up to five. The door opened slightly above the level of the floor, so they alighted into the apartment. Excited, she went to the windows and looked out. It was a nice street with lovely houses. She walked out the front door and into the yard. She turned and saw the modest white house she had just left. Then she scanned the street again. Exactly what fifth floor is this?

Meg woke up perplexed. She bypassed making the coffee and walked to the corner of the room she used as an office. She stood directly in front of a large bookcase and ran her fingers up and down a stack of books until she found the one she wanted. She opened it in the middle and then thumbed back to the chapter, accurately named, "The 'F's.'" She scanned the page until she came to "Five: See numbers." She flipped forward until she found the "N's" and then "Numbers." She sat down and read: "The number five is the number of man, forming a pentagon, being endless, and the power of the circle. Like the circle, the pentacle symbolizes the whole and the meeting points of heaven and earth. Five is also the marriage number of the *hieros gamos* as the combination of the feminine, even, number two, and the masculine, odd, number three."

"Hmm," she thought. She closed the book and went to make coffee.

She woke up the next morning, dreamless, but with a pit in her stomach. It had been over ten years and she was still having trouble swallowing. Her best friend, Mary, told her that meant congestion in her throat chakra. Swallowing was the bridge between the head and the heart. Her head told her to move on; her heart was still having trouble reconciling it.

It was impossible for her to feel what she supposed everyone else felt. For fifty years she had tried to imitate how everyone else acted, how everyone else talked, how everyone else conducted daily life. Now she not only failed at being like them, but also like herself. It was as if she wore a lie tattooed on her soul.

Chorus: "She cries to the heavens. There is a stone in my head. I don't appear to be thinking straight anymore. She cries to the Gods. There is a spasm in my heart. I don't appear to be feeling anymore. What do I know? The sun gives me relief, the night brings me chills. She cries into the empty void. There is strangeness to my days. I know I eat, I know I smile, I know I move about and I know I talk. But when I sleep it is forgotten and the mystic world I return to is my comfort, my sanctuary, my home.

So she cries to her angels, "Please protect me because I am walking on the glass fence between here and there and I know which side I should jump to but it is not the side I'd like to be on."

Mary tells her it's dangerous to play this game. "Death is just a matter of taking the next exit. We can choose," she said. Meg's not sure this fact consoles her.

The alarm clocks buzzes and she reaches over to turn it off. She yawns and puts her forearm over her eyes. Was that a dream within the dream she just had? Was Mary in the dream or did Mary really tell her that?

The dog yawns, making funny gurgling sounds as he opens his mouth. He stretches then nervously starts pacing the room. She knows he wants to go outside and start his day. She decides she'd better start hers as well.

She swings her legs over the bed and her right foot lands directly on a blob of green goo. Instinctively, she recoils and as she jerks her leg up and away; the goo goes flying off her foot willy-nilly. Some of it lands on the wall and starts slithering towards the floor. She panics for a moment; has she just stepped on some weird insect? She notices a minute trace of blob on her thigh. She peers down at it. Upon closer reflection, there are small, brown specks interspersed in the green, gelatinous substance. Certainly not an insect, she decides. For some reason, this makes her feel less queasy.

She gets out of bed and hops on the left and unsullied foot, across the wooden floor, towards the bathroom. She stumbles and smacks her right foot on the floor. She gives up and trails smudged green footprints behind her. She pretends not to notice.

Minutes later, she comes out of the bathroom, a fluffy towel wrapped around her midsection, another poised in her hand to wipe up the mess. The room is spotless. Not a trace of green goo anywhere. The dog stands in the doorway begging to be let out.

"Balthazar, did you eat that stuff on the floor?" she says. The dog yawns and gurgles some more.

Narrator: "As we know, time is a set of numbers, an abstraction that humans devised to keep civilization going. GMT, the Earth's timepiece, was voted on in 1884 to keep the world orderly and our clocks in sync. Time keeps everything from happening at once. Einstein thought that time denotes relationships of changes in the universe and nothing else.

So the argument is: Does time really exist at all? Or is it a fundamental part of the cosmos?"

Meg pauses as the bell tower in the courtyard rings out, announcing the next class change. Her boss, Mr. Monahan, looks at his oversized watch and then glances at the clock on the wall.

He squints, "A few minutes off, it is."

He clicks his tongue in disapproval just as the clock audibly ticks the next minute off in protest. Mr. Monahan stares at nothing for a second as if he's lost his thoughts.

"No matter," he says. He stands and looks down at her. "Meg, you agree, don't you? We must finish the proposal 'tout de suite'?"

She nods her agreement but before she can speak, he turns and hurries away.

"No matter," she says.

She gathers her notebooks, her phone, and her satchel. The minute hand sticks at the twelve, making a loud buzzing sound before it pulls itself free and continues its way around the plane of the clock. It is exactly five past five.

Chorus: "She lives an exemplary life, one of hard work, kindness and purpose. She has searched for the truth to know what she couldn't remember. Now that she has found it, she wants to go back to not knowing. But that is impossible. The universe doesn't work that way. The thought is now thought. The intention is now out."

Mary is jogging around Meg's driveway as she pulls in. She is dressed in a pink tracksuit, and white tennis shoes with a multi-colored ski hat pulled down tightly over her ears. The pom-poms on her ski hat float loosely behind her as if two miniature furbies have decided to come out and play. She sports a serious looking pedometer clipped to the waistband of her pants.

Meg rushes out of the car to her front door, arms laden with work accoutrements.

She yells over her shoulder. "Sorry I'm late, Mare. It'll take just a second," she says. She fiddles around in her purse, tipping it to the right and the left. "Damn keys are always at the bottom," she mumbles.

Out of exasperation, she dumps her armload to the ground and looks in earnest for the keys. She stops and thinks, then reaches into her coat and extracts the silver ring. She lifts it in the air and shakes it.

"Now doesn't get any better than this," Mary says. She takes an ex-aggerated gulp of air and pumps her arms. "I've already clocked a whopping 1,640 steps."

CHAPTER TWO

In her dream a man was pulling large numbers out of the air and eating them. In particular, he was ate the number two and three.

Meg woke up and groaned.

"Five? Again?" she said. She punched the pillow in the empty space next to her. "Couldn't it be a seven or an eight?"

She leaned over the bed and looked at Balthazar, who was lying on a blanket, staring pensively at her. "Whatcha think? A four, like you? Or maybe a two? I know! How about a one? One *is* the loneliest number, you know."

She laughed at her own joke and Balthazar wagged his tail. She started to get out of bed and hesitated. She scanned the floor. All clean. She looked around the room. All the same as she remembered.

Satisfied, she got out of bed and headed for the shower, humming the song, "One is the Loneliest Number," as she went. Balthazar got up and stretched. He trotted after her, a little dollop of green goo sticking to his tail.

Narrator: Temporal Dislocation is a term to explain that the past, present and future exist all at once, they are all happening now. We rarely think that way because different moments of time exist somewhere else and not with us. Therefore, our human experience keeps us cloistered and naively thinking what we experience is universal.

One theory, noted by Brian Greene, would be that on the deepest levels of reality, each moment is an intense snapshot. How objects relate to one another, waves crashing on the beach, for example, are snapshots within snapshots that are not in communication with one another. But rather the brain assembles these snaps (such as twenty-four frames per second) to create movement.

Therefore, nothing changes, all exists simultaneously. Does the number seven say the number six has died?

So then you must ask, "Why does time matter?"

PART V

MONEY

RODGER JACOBS

THE AIR DOWN THERE

Earl pocketed the nine dollars and ten cents and spit on a pile of scrap aluminum to show his displeasure.

"You saying that's all what the brass and copper in that thing is worth?" Earl scowled.

The recycling dealer never liked Earl. He had the hooked nose and beady eyes of a predatory bird and his clothing always smelled of beer and Wonder Bread. But what he disliked even more than Earl was so-called "modern" or "abstract" art. Destroying those tangled heaps of twisted metal was a personal fetish and Earl was his enabler. Stupid Earl who wouldn't know a Jackson Pollock from a velvet Elvis.

"The effort alone to get that thing out of the storage yard is worth fifty bucks," Earl protested.

"This is a metal recycling center, Earl. I pay for the content, not for your time and effort. If that's what you're lacking, get a job that pays wages."

There was an old wood-frame church across the street from the recycling center on Wilmington Boulevard, right smack dab in the shadow of one of the thirteen refineries that churn out millions of barrels of oil a day and leave the air down there thick with the sickly sweet smell of gasoline.

It was Sunday so there was hymnal singing going on in the church and it carried in the emission-laden air to Earl's ears where it made a most unpleasant noise.

"Hey-a, Pete—?" he called after the dealer, who had turned his back on Earl and was trudging back to the small shack that was his office. "He's got one in his storage yard that's ten feet."

Pete paused in the dirt pathway and kicked at a mound of swarming red ants. "How d'you know it's ten feet?"

"Measured it," Earl announced proudly. "Measured it with a tape measure."

"Uh-huh. And what's it look like?"

"Like all the rest of the stuff, Pete. Garbage."

Pete understood that an Abraham Verton sculpture of that size would probably fetch twenty-nine thousand dollars from a collector.

Tearing down an abomination like that would provide Pete with an almost orgasmic thrill. Who was Verton anyway? A nobody. He never studied art like Pete once had. Abraham Verton was a seventy-year-old black man, a retired welder who still liked to tinker around with a torch and metal. He was something of a folk hero in South Central all because someone paid five grand for one of his tangled pieces of junk and before you knew it an "artist" was born, a regular Grandma Moses from Watts.

"I'll give you a hundred for it," Pete said in a voice that did not invite debate

"Jesus, Pete." Earl hooked his thumbs in the belt loops of his jeans and inched them up over his beer gut. "The old man's put up razor wire on his fence and he's bolted the sculptures down. Next thing you know he's gonna buy a guard dog. I swear to it. He will."

"Two hundred."

The church choir across the street stopped praising God in ear-splitting song. With the sudden silence Earl felt a vague emotion come over him.

"It was on the TV, you know. On the news." Earl said. "They said he was dying of cancer and isn't it all terrible that someone is breaking into his storage yard and stealing his stuff. And I know, Pete, 'cause of what I heard on the news. I know what these hunks of junk're worth and you best start paying me better or I return to bringing you beer cans."

Pete gave Earl's challenge the gravest consideration. He couldn't pay Earl one-tenth of what a Verton was worth. But for the sheer pleasure of reducing another one to scrap he would now have to dig a little deeper in his wallet.

"Tell you what," he said, shifting on his feet like a shy dancer. "Bring me the ten-footer and I'll give you two hundred and I'll throw in a twelve-pack of Tecate."

"Miller Genuine Draft," Earl countered.

"Done deal."

Earl scratched his rear end through the seat of his pants and ambled back to his white utility truck parked near the gate. He was a gifted haggler, just like his dad.

AL BASILE

HOW I LEARNED THE VALUE OF MONEY

The spare but clean front room was brown on brown
and drab on plain to me, yet opulence,
hard won by thirty rugged years of labor
to him, who'd come here from the old country.
He couldn't speak my English, but he'd gestured—
his thickened hand had poked, to show me, twice.
A boy, I left the tiny kitchen where
my mother's aunts would serve pizzelles, and pour
the thumb-sized drams of anisette, and stepped
into the sitting room for the first time.
The dull, correct white curtains let in light.
The Sunday morning street beyond was still.

Mass over, we were visiting. The short
old man was right behind me, peering down
without his glasses, and a chain led from
a button on his black vest, over to
one pocket, where its gold links disappeared.
I wondered why Ziu Brazzi brought me here—
we couldn't really talk—but then he made
a face I saw was serious, and reached
into the other pocket of his vest
with his left hand, then pulled it out and turned
it over. Dimes and nickels in his palm,
from Mercury to Buffalo, looked out
at me like muffins through the oven glass.

He looked at them a long time. Could he see
them well enough? Details were clear to me;
I read dates from the twenties easily.
The objects in his hand—were they a blur
to him, blank discs of different sizes? Was
he trying to identify their value?
Or was he turning over in his mind
how much to give me? For I realized
now that this was ritual, and private.

➢

At last his thumb and forefinger came down,
both blunted by shoe factory machines
and years of piece work in the shops, and picked
a nickel to present to me. I guessed,
the way a kid will do, that he had got
it wrong, and thought it was a quarter—
I carefully accepted, so he'd see
I understood the value of his gift,
but I was disappointed, secretly.

That nickel is long spent, for penny candy.
There was a shop across from grammar school.
The counter girl held out her palm, next to
the licorice jar; the nickel disappeared.
But richer now, I see what it was worth.

CONRAD ROMO

PILLOW TALK

Gilbert and I tip back and guzzle our fake beers as we take in a pole dance. We lean our backs against the bar. Strippers grind to a blaring 70s rock song. We each hold our bottles palming the label to conceal the fact that the piss we drink is non-alcoholic, not that anyone's looking. It's dark in the club and all the light and attention is pointed towards the stage. But, still, we both have our pride.

Gilbert and I met in an AA meeting. It was a round robin type where everyone sits in a circle and has to share for a couple of minutes. When it was my turn, I talked about being new to town, that I had a couple of years plus of sobriety and was looking forward to a new start and hoped one day to call myself *a sourdough*. The *sourdough* thing I heard was what Alaskans called people that stuck it out during the winter instead of those that took off to the lower forty-eight at the first sign of frost.

Someone snickered and said: *One winter at a time, Bud.*

After the meeting, Gilbert introduced himself and asked if I wanted to grab a bite and a little fellowship. That was two months ago and since then we've become regulars at this particular strip club. AA dogma says that you shouldn't go into bars unless you have some specific business there. Our *business*, we justified, was that we were hungry. A topless waitress with a green Mohawk who goes by the name of Pillow brings us our order of burritos. They've got decent Mexican— and decent Mexican tastes better looking at naked women.

He tilts his head towards me and says out of the side of his mouth, "*Jesse, do you know anything about pyramid games?*"

"*A little,*" I answer with my mouth full of carnitas.

He has no idea that a main reason I had to get out of L.A. and wound up in Anchorage was because of trouble I got into from pyramid games.

Without asking me what I know, Gilbert explains the basics while we keep our eyes on the talent. I don't interrupt in case there is a new wrinkle that I hadn't worked before.

The way it works is simple, he says. You buy in at the bottom for a hundred or a thousand or five. Say we're talking about a five-thousand-dollar pyramid. Okay? You got sixteen squares on the bottom, eight above that, four above that, then two, and then one at the top. Follow? You buy a square at the bottom and twenty-five hundred dollars goes to the person right above you and the other twenty-five hundred dollars goes to the top position. Okay? Once all sixteen spots on the bottom are full, the top guy has gotten paid forty thousand dollars plus the twenty-five hundred dollars that he got back when he was in the second level. Now everyone moves up to the next level, so the two guys on the second level now are at the top as the pyramid splits and they start collecting. Sweet huh?

I nod my head and wipe my mouth on a napkin as Pillow takes the stage and works the pole, pointing her ass in our direction.

Pyramid games were indirectly why I was in Alaska. I could attest that pyramid games work, particularly if you are in the first rush, which I was. And, better yet, if you start your own and conveniently put your name or your partner's on top, which I did. Eventually they all come to a grinding halt. They always do and a lot of people will lose their money and get resentful and look for someone to blame. A few people back in LA wanted to hurt me so it seemed like a good idea to leave. I had blown whatever money I had earned from the pyramid games, but I had enough for a plane ticket and I knew someone who knew someone who made me offer to crew in the Bering Strait for Dungeness crab. I just had to get a job in a canning factory first, so that I got used to the long eighteen-hour days, and then work on a salmon boat so I got my sea legs and then I'd have a job on a crab boat waiting for me. I got the job in the cannery out of the way, but once I had a few thousand in hand, the stories of extreme danger that I kept hearing about the high seas got to me and I decided to stay on land and to hell with the Bering Strait.

Gilbert was all wound up about a pyramid meeting he'd been to the day before.

"I saw a guy cash out with forty thousand!" he said.

"How many people were there?"

"The place was packed, maybe close to fifty, I dunno," he said.

It would take time to get it worked out and how to make him think it was all his idea would be part of the equation. Time was all I needed. Time to patiently think it through. Alaska was an expensive place to live and the potential cash in a room like the one Gilbert described had me forming a whole other idea.

A Teena Marie song was playing. Pillow was still on stage. I remembered her once telling me *Teena Marie makes, me proud to be white!* I looked at Gilbert fixated on Pillow. He drained the remains of his bottle. On his right knuckles were the letters M-E-R-C-Y.

He hadn't decided what to put on the other hand yet.

PART VI

WATER

DONNA HILBERT

THE SWIMMER

Brown hair stuffed in a cap
strapped under my chin, I swam
through junior high summers
at the Reseda Park pool,
in water heavy with chlorine.
All summer I smelled
like the sink
Mother sprinkled with Comet
before leaving for work.

Maxine's mom was a dry cleaner.
Days off, she cadged
invitations to swim
in backyard pools of the rich
whose clothes she pressed,
steamed in her shop.
Mother said she was nervy
just like Maxine. Like Maxine,
her hair was curly, dark.

Days after swimming,
we dipped crackers
in mustard, Worcestershire,
any liquid found in their kitchen
went into our sauce,
an extra-strength potion.
We dipped, ate, were transformed
into amazing girls:
scientists, swimmers.

At school in September:
Whose tan is darkest?
Which camp is better,
Malibu, Pine Flats?
I longed to be one of *them*
a Valerie or Susan,
whose long blonde hair
turned green every summer.

GERARD MANLEY HOPKINS

HEAVEN HAVEN

I have desired to go
Where springs not fail,
To fields where flies no sharp and sided hail,
And a few lilies blow.

And I have asked to be
Where no storms come,
Where the green swell is in the havens dumb,
And out of the swing of the sea.

Ruth Moon Kempher

GREEN DAY, SURFSIDE

gilt-fingered seaoats wagging

where pastel houses crouch

tight-shuttered, in the dunes

walking the dogs, we watch

as jets embroider above us

white fluff lines across

faded green denim, their

warnings threaten, spreading

white duck-down: once home

we find that storm, a pressure

curled like a comma, in a green-

glass ampule, signal of doom.

BARBARA EKNOIAN

LAKE HOPATCONG

It was more than a summer place,
the lake with its many coves.
I'd drift in the rowboat
in front of my favorite house
painted aquamarine
with double-decked porches.
The steady slip slap sounds
of easy waves splashing
against the boat calmed me.
I was away from trouble back home.

I used to pretend that some day
I would live in a lakefront home
with a sprawling green lawn
and a hammock tied
between two lean trees,
where I'd read books,
then stroll down to the dock
and dip my feet into the water.

The summer days stretched
to infinity while my cares
melted in the summer sun.
Then I'd row the boat
under the River Styx Bridge
past diners on the patio
of the Bon Aire Hotel
and on to Byram's Cove.

I want to row away to that place
where green trees shade
and water shines in the sunlight
enticing me to live happily
in the pastel aquamarine house.

PATRICK DELANEY

SPRING RAIN

Steam rises like smoke from the sidewalks and street as the wind chases the low black clouds across the sky in front of me. They look so close that I might touch one. Sitting with my bare feet up on the old metal chair in the dark shade of the front porch, everything is in black and white. I watch a single leaf whip through the air like a kite on a string. The sun bursts from the clouds, turning the leaf a bright green before it shrinks away from me. Stepping off the porch, the last of the rain trickles from the downspouts, as everything explodes in color. I can smell the shingles on the roof as they start to heat up. Standing in the sun with my eyes closed, the cars whizzing past on the wet street sound like waves splashing on the beach, and I pretend to be down the shore.

I hear the squealing of brakes and the loud hinges of a car door opening in front of the house, and I know before looking it's Uncle Larry. He slides across the front seat of his faded black Chevrolet with no hubcaps and out the passenger side door like someone in an old movie. Drenched from delivering the mail in the rain, he pushes through the rusty gate between the hedges and runs straight into the house without saying a word.

It's getting hotter and the grass and the hedges look like they're growing right in front of me. The humming of the pumps and the suck-ing of water start to come from the backyard that is the swamp, Uncle Larry's swamp. I hear the sound of the metal bolt on the door of the back porch, then the door opening. Standing in the doorway is Uncle Larry in big black heavy boots that reach to the bottom of his checkered shorts. His sleeveless white undershirt shows the hair on his arms and shoulders that I think all black-haired men must have. He peers out through his black-rimmed glasses looking right past me as he adjusts his blue safari helmet still wet from delivering mail all morning in the rain.

I watch him as he starts down the steps in his shiny rubber boots that he orders out of the Sears and Roebuck catalogue. I remember him tearing the whole page out and circling the boots with a red crayon be-fore handing it to Aunt Grace. On the day they come in the mail, he rips the big box open and holds the boots above his head. "Look at 'em," he says. "They're perfect." That night, he eats supper with the boots on.

Now he squeaks his way to the top of the hill above the swamp. Standing with his legs spread wide, he tilts back the helmet before putting both hands on his hips. I move in slow behind him, staying close to the house, along the warm damp walkway. The stiff grey electric cord hangs out of the back porch window that hinges at the top and is propped open from the bottom with a piece of wood. The cord dangles above the swamp on metal clothesline poles and stretches to a wooden post sticking out of the mud and water below. Four large pumps connected by extension cords and duct tape plug into an outlet nailed to the post.

Clumps of long sharp grass shoot up from pools of water and tiger lilies spread out everywhere. Brown punks reach out from the water like great big corn dogs on a stick. The giant willow tree hisses in the hot wind as Uncle Larry wades into the water like a trapper, moving the first pump into the deepest section of the swamp. The slurping and gurgling sound puts a smile on his face, and I think now that I am invisible to him. I glide past him along the side of the yard through the clear water, looking at my feet disappear into the grass below, churning up mud with each step.

"What do you think you're doin'?" he says, stopping me in my tracks.

My feet feel like a hundred pounds each as I turn around to face him. I don't say a word and feel shorter than usual. We just stare at each other standing in the water. It seems like minutes passing, until he takes off his helmet and pulls a red bandana out of the pocket of his shorts and wipes his forehead like he's in a real swamp.

"Watch yourself," he says, as he turns away and trudges to the next pump.

What does he mean by that, I wonder. Watch myself in the swamp because he thinks it's dangerous or just watch myself?

I climb up onto the hood of the old abandoned green car that looks like its growing out of the swamp behind the willow tree. It has the look of an old tank left to rot after a lost battle. Uncle Larry is talking to himself in a low voice as he shakes the pumps around. It sounds like he's explaining the whole operation to someone, but I can't hear who.

Lying back against the windshield, I see him putting the hoses from the pumps into the long black pipe that runs all the way to the back road—the whole time pointing and talking to someone who isn't there. Not for real, anyway. The water starts to run out across the road and into the creek. He follows the moving water to the end of the pipe and stares at it empting into the creek. I slide off the hood between the car and the tree out of his sight, careful not to get too close to the tree because its trunk is wrapped in poison oak.

Uncle Larry has a long walking stick that he carries around in the swamp to poke around with, ever since he found out John Sabacas from up the street put two rat snakes in here last summer. Sometimes he holds the stick under his arm like a gun, and I wonder if he pretends it is a rifle. When he takes a break, he rests his helmet on top of it. As it pokes out of the mud, he wipes his face and head with the bandana like a solider in the jungle.

Deiterly, the scrap man, comes over and laughs at Uncle Larry because he uses the pumps to get rid of the water. He tells him, "You can do that all day, every day, and you're still gonna have water in that yard. There are underground springs and you know it for Christ's sake."

Uncle Larry just ignores him and, as the water slows down, walks back to move the pumps again. He says he won't give him the satisfaction, but I think he's afraid on account of Mr. Deiterly being so big and all. He calls him Lerch because he looks like the giant butler on the *Addam's Family*, but he doesn't say it to his face.

Back up on the car, I watch the dragonflies hover around the swamp like helicopters in Vietnam, where my cousin Joe, the Marine, is right now. I once heard Joe call his father Don Quixote when he sees him out back and says the pumps are his windmills, whatever that means.

Aunt Grace tells her husband, "You're doin' a good job out there, Larry. As soon as you get it dry enough, I'll start hanging laundry out there." I see her laughing at him from the kitchen window, and I know she's making fun of him. I don't like either of them, but I hate it when she does that to him. He doesn't say anything to her, nothing at all. He just takes it, but he has the swamp that's bright and beautiful, and all she has is the television that's black and white.

I think he lets me hang around at a distance because he knows I'm the one who understands it. Me and the cat, that is. Killer is Uncle Larry's sidekick in the swamp. He comes meowing out of the brush like a tiger and rubs up against Uncle Larry's black boots before following his master around the swamp. After a few rounds, he stretches out on a small patch of high ground right in the middle of everything and rests with his head up and his eyes closed. Uncle Larry stands next to him as if he has befriended a big cat in the wild, as he holds the walking stick under his arm like a weapon. I watch the two of them from the hood of the car and think that right now standing in the sun in the middle of the swamp surrounded by a sea of green he is as free and happy as the cat and that is pretty good.

After a few hours, the humming of the pumps has stopped and I feel exposed on the car for the first time. I slide back down into the soggy grass and walk to the end of the long black pipe at the edge of the back road. The water has stopped and I see Uncle Larry moving up to the house. I keep my eyes on him, until he disappears onto the back porch, and I think maybe he's wondering when it will rain again.

Marc Malandra

LEAVING PACIFIC GROVE

1.
Land's end—
gulls on an updraft, trawlers
setting out to gather shrimp—
I had something to say.
Jade sea unsaid it.

2.
A stink bug labors over a leaf.
Seals bake, far, furred sausages on the rocks.
An otter daydreams on a bed of kelp.
A raven's shrill reveille, gull cries, rushing
tides sighing and crumpling over seaweed;
one last afternoon educated at my leisure.

3.
If I stay here to watch pines
twist into limbs, sap-strong
yet seeming-rotten, would I learn
language wind uses to entice
clouds into apparition?
If I strip fears like bark
from these trees will the exposed self
stand salt blasts and flood rains?
Am I less myself when divided
or more myself when less
the sum of my parts, some
of my parts tree-like, rock-
like, though less noble?

4.
I'm looking at my cloud-self
as it passes over a pool,
over chance-grasping anemones.
I'm thinking about surfaces,
how far down I have to look.

5.
A white dove arcs over the cove.
A raven scavenges among the rocks,
strutting bundle of tar with wings.
Shards of light, sand, and stone oscillate,
scenes from the life of saint
change, patron of tides. Wind
ripples the inlet into mosaic.

GAIA HOLMES

BEACHCOMBER

There was never any danger
in her life
but everything she picked
and pocketed from the tide line
was broken and dreamed of biting:
Whimbrels' bills, the jagged necks
of Jim Beam bottles,
gulls eggs, fluted clavicles
and slack crabs claws.

The horizons
of her landscapes
were full of holes.
Buds shriveled and flaked
before they had time
to bloom.
Wonky suns slipped
down the skies,
cracked and seeped
their broken golds
across her crayoned fields.

She was one of those girls
who Sellotaped crushed moths
into her school-books,
one of those girls
who let fruit rot in her satchel
before it ripened,
one of those girls
who scrawled her anxiety
into wet cement
and left it to set.

AMY LOWELL

THE GREEN BOWL

This little bowl is like a mossy pool
In a Spring wood, where dogtooth violets grow
Nodding in chequered sunshine of the trees;
A quiet place, still, with the sound of birds,
Where, though unseen, is heard the endless song
And murmur of the never resting sea.
'Twas winter, Roger, when you made this cup,
But coming Spring guided your eager hand
And round the edge you fashioned young green leaves,
A proper chalice made to hold the shy
And little flowers of the woods. And here
They will forget their sad uprooting, lost
In pleasure that this circle of bright leaves
Should be their setting; once more they will dream
They hear winds wandering through lofty trees
And see the sun smiling between the leaves.

MARCIA MEARA

ON THE RIVER

Crystal green flows beneath me,
Leafy arches rise above.
  Dip, glide.
    Dip, glide.
      Slide.

Duckweed parts as I float by.
I wonder where they went,
Those ducks?
Gone overnight, it seems.
Another parting, another loss,
And I slide by,
Under all that green.
  Dip, glide.
    Dip, glide.

Just there, in deepest shade,
Sleeping emeralds cling.
Tree frogs rest in their
Smooth, damp skins
Waiting for the silver moon.
They'll open their eyes for the silver moon.
Sleeping now,
As I pass by.
  Dip, glide.
    Dip, glide.

With arms raised to that same moon,
I once danced along the shore,
Young and wild and full of joy.
Moving to music
That stirred my soul,
And washed in that pale light,
I danced.
Years ago, in that pale, pale light.
I remember it all,
And so much more,
As I slide by.
  Dip, glide.
    Dip, glide.

A scaled ribbon of vivid lime
Scribbles across my bow,

Curving by in his own silent slide.
I smile at Dickinson's "narrow fellow"
Tasting the air with his tongue of flame.
I feel no "zero at the bone" for him,
For I have known far worse than he,
And survived.
With a nod of my head,
I pass him, too,
And on I go.
  Dip, glide.
    Dip, glide.

Time and time and time goes by,
And still, green fronds protect me from above,
Green water lifts me from below,
Carrying me ceaselessly on my way.
Slower, now that Youth is gone,
Yet, sometimes a froth of foam and spray
Reminds me of those early days,
When all the water rushed clear and cold,
And teemed with Promise so bright
You could almost catch it in your hands.
That bubbling spring where it all began
Now lies so far behind.
Far behind, and long ago,
While I move on.
  Dip, glide.
    Dip, glide.

Always forward,
One stroke at a time,
The only path from Here to There.
One stroke following another,
And I, all the while,
Still cherish the trees above,
The water below.
I wonder as a turn grows near,
What adventures wait beyond the bend?
Will they make my heart beat fast again?
How many shimmering curves lie before me yet?
How long does my river flow?
  Dip, glide.
    Dip, glide.
      Dip, glide.
        Slide.

JOE HAKIM

LILY POND

In the autumn of
the last year when I
felt the need
to know everything
about everything,
I had the power
to turn gardens into
battlefields—
I could
conquer entire worlds
by the side of a privet hedge
and steer the journey
of a legend
with the tip of
a branch.

Until one day,
at Grandma Simpkin's
house, where I had
colonised the edge
of a lily pond at the
foot of her garden.
It was to be the harbour from
which I would launch
an assault into a
neighbouring land, and
as I prepared my army to
embark on a voyage
across a
dirty green ocean,

I slipped and
fell in,
fell into
the putrid, filthy
water. Submerged,
I thrashed
around and cried for someone

to save me, but
my battalions stood mute
and immobile and
watched my struggle
with moulded plastic
indifference.

As my nostrils and mouth
and ears
filled up, I screamed and
spluttered, as a
a dark
liquid
panic swept over
me, a feeling I had never
experienced before,
and then a hand grabbed
my wrist and
Grandma Simpkin
pulled me out.

As I stood
by her fire, naked and
shivering under a blanket,
trying to shake
all the bits of weed
and dirt
and leaves
out of my head,
I began to understand
something:

At some point in my life,
I would
die
and there was nothing
I could do about it.

CHRIS DAVIDSON

AUBADE

In the morning ocean, a gray a shade
darker than the sky, a fin rose
and repeatedly sank in the same patch
of water, for a minute or two,
then vanished, and the water where
the fin had been recovered its shape,
like a rift in the earth repaired
by a movement of earth.

The bodiless voice with me
on the drive to the beach said
the tundras melt, the seas rise.
The fish, wrapped in water, trapped
between earth and sun, are akin
to you, my consuming fire, young,
home, wrapped in your bed asleep,
a-swim and for now unchained.

IVON PREFONTAINE

WHAT CAN I DO?

On a sombre day—
Grief and sorrow the order,
A message heard:
Change begins in me.
I am a catalyst
I look inside:
Call forth a gentle spirit–
Give it voice.
In light, love happens—
Resonates,
Reaches out its hand
Beckons others join.
Rings on clearest pond,
Ripples of love touch,
Right cascades forth,
Good people meet.
Good touches good,
Prayer meets prayer,
Love conquers hate
Join together.
Good people summoned—
Their tears catalyze,
Grieve and heal as one,
We are change.
Be a community–
It is not a distant loss:
It is our loss—
Feel it.
Small change is ours—
We each contribute,
Love multiplies:
Heals the world.

PART VII

SEASONS

STEVEN KUHN

SPRING CLEANING

Out of this house,
out of this heart's silent chambers
ordered through sludge and past offenses
ordered to report to light,
he yet drags his feet.

In the Spring,
there are colors that have been forgotten
and
there are hatches long rusted shut-
there is water to be let in.

Where once music leapt like
rainstorm frogs
now just words, phrases, fragments
occasionally whip around
chalky metal corners
to spook him. To make him remember.

GAIA HOLMES

THE GLASS HOUSE

Winter has sucked the landscape
back to black and white
but in the glass house
the world is plump and curved,
full of juice and spectrums.

We sit on the edge
of the vicious garden
where tropical flowers
shred the light with their teeth.
The steamy scent
of sap and green life
soaks through our coats
and makes us sweat.

In here, nothing is subtle.
Hungry proboscis leer
and lick the balmy air.
Colours pulse, drip and dazzle.
Petals do not drift or whisper,
they drop onto the dirt
with a succulent thud:
He loves me, he loves me not.

Later I will remember
the languid names of plants
that kill with sweetness;
Nepenthes, Pinguicula, Saracenia.
I will think of those gentle Latin nouns
turning into sensuous verbs
and I will think of him,
his shy soapstone fingers
turning into claws.

From *Lifting The Piano With One Hand*
(Comma Press, Spring 2013)

Benjamin Myers

THE SEASONS CHANGE LIKE A WOMAN IN HER EARLY 30s
PREPARING TO MEET A MAN FOR ONLY THEIR THIRD DATE

The seasons change like a woman
in her early 30s preparing to meet
a new man for only their third date.

They will eat, they will drink,
they will laugh; her wrists and
ears are perfumed with stringent musk.

Yesterday was winter but tomorrow
will be spring and her mattress is one thousand
daffodil bulbs deep in the soil of longing.

JERI THOMPSON

WAITING FOR GREEN

Especially the trees

Stripped of their fleshy garments

Shudder in this chill.

Under the winter cold

My bones are reminded they are brittle things

Like the leaves under my feet.

As I wait for green

To awaken under a March sun

I reminisce about sunsets after 8 pm,

Sweating in the dry August air,

And trees dressed in their finest attire

Strutting in the afternoon breeze,

Happy to no longer be naked

In the face of this heartless winter's gaze.

SANDYLEE MACCOBY

EMMA GREEN

At Greenhill, the teachers run around in flats or sneakers except for Martha, their glamorous principal, and members of the foreign language department who wears elegant clothes and accessories from Paris and Milan. Emma Green always dresses for school in her old college jeans and green sweaters as though she were still a high school student. Some of her eighth grade boys get crushes on her until she tells them she's twenty-four years old!

Her green sweaters emphasize the emerald green of her eyes and though she is called Emma, her real name is Emerald, taken from "The Emerald Island," the birthplace of her ancestors: the lush, green island of Ireland.

When Emma started teaching Art in the Middle School at Greenhill two years before, she was impressed how quickly the kids picked up on her message of spontaneity in making art. Not too much detail and staying abstract. Right away she plastered the lobby walls with their work and who knows? Any one of those kids could be the next Frankenthaler or Andy Warhol.

Her ex-boyfriend, Bob, was now a well-known writer, but when she'd lived with him he was a frustrated accountant. One day he headed for the library instead of the office and wrote the first of a bestselling series of children's books about a little frog whose home on the river is destroyed by runoff from a field drenched in pesticides, and who is rescued by a crowd of beavers who live in a three-story fortress of logs.

Emma was glad Bob had done so well with his stories, but it was she who'd initiated their breakup. Bob was the strong, silent type who liked to scuba dive so he could escape the world of people, and she was lonely, searching for someone who enjoyed talking just for the fun of it.

The disruptive antics of her young students were a constant challenge for her, and she could never get it right. She was either too indulgent or excessively punitive.

Teaching art was messy with all the paints, glue, and scissors, and after each class she was down on her knees, picking up trash and torn paper. Though she always reminded the kids to clean up after themselves before they left the room, they were out the door before she could catch them.

One rainy day, the history teacher, George Ryan, who had recently become head of the middle school, dropped by the art room to observe

Emma's eighth grade class. Had he heard she couldn't control the kids? Maybe somebody from the art department tipped him off because it was true. She no longer tried to get a noisy class to settle down and wished she had learned sign language because that would have quieted the kids right away. She'd seen it work in the D.C. public schools, where some of the teachers taught the kids sign language and a whole classroom fell silent. When a student needed to go to the bathroom, he signed the request with his fingers and the teacher signed back. Sign language had great appeal: no reading, no writing, and, best of all, no talking.

Emma believed that Greenhill should be teaching sign language as well as French, Spanish, and Chinese.

George Ryan stood outside her classroom for at least ten minutes before entering, and she wondered what he was doing there all that time. Most likely, he was listening to the noise emanating from her class and when he did come in, his expression smacked of disapproval and annoyance. When a teacher was young and inexperienced like Emma, it was his job to intervene and help—and, at heart, he wasn't a helper.

Emma was certain something awful was about to happen—she could feel it in her bones—and she was right. Ronny, a hyperactive boy of fourteen, giggling hysterically while the other kids formed a circle around him, jumped out of his seat and started scribbling dirty words all over his painting with a red magic marker. She yelled at him to stop, but he paid no attention and egged on by the kids, continued writing. Then George Ryan switched off the ceiling lights and in a thunderous voice ordered the class to be quiet. Quickly sneaking back to his desk, Ronny sat down and watched as the kids sheepishly returned to their seats. An eerie silence engulfed the room and George Ryan turned to Emmy and said sharply, "Come to my office, Miss Green. 12:00." After he was gone, the kids broke out into derisive laughter. "You're in trouble, Miss Green! You're in trouble!" they cried. Tears of shame rolled down her cheeks and she ran outside in the hall to get control of herself. She must not let the children see her pain.

Exactly at noon, she knocked on George Ryan's door. There was no response so she knocked again, louder, and called out his name. "Mr. Ryan?" Was he napping? After all, he was no longer a young man, late forties, at least. Finally, she shoved open the heavy door and there he was, sitting at his desk by the window at the far end of the room, staring straight at her, his face expressionless. When she approached him, he made no effort to greet her. She noticed that his desk was clear of its usual books or piles of papers and its smooth wooden surface gleamed in the light. A dark, abstract painting hung on the wall behind his desk.

Her voice shaking, she said, "You wanted to see me, Mr. Ryan?"

His dark eyes flashed and he nodded. "Yes, " he said.

Sinking down in the chair beside his desk, she burst into loud sobs. "What should I have done? Please tell me!"

"You have very little experience, Emma. You are quite green. A few years in the classroom should do the trick."

"But I couldn't control myself! They could see I was crying so I had to run out of the room!"

"No need to worry, Miss Green. It actually might be a good thing for the kids to know their behavior can affect a grownup to that degree."

"Really? Oh, I do feel better, hearing you say that." She gave him a wan smile and he found himself softening towards her, stirred by her limpid green eyes, her youth, and her vulnerability.

A silence fell and Emma saw through the window that the buds were opening up on the trees and thick new grass was growing on the soccer field. Spring was here and she hadn't even realized it.

"Who's the teacher?" Mr. Ryan was saying.

"What?"

"Who's the teacher?" he repeated.

Her mind went blank. The painting on the wall behind him upset her. Was that a younger face of Mr. Ryan behind the dark brown and green streaks of paint?

"Am I looking at a portrait of you?" she asked, her green eyes wide with curiosity.

"Yes, by the Brooklyn artist, Saul Minoleto," said Mr. Ryan proudly. "Clever of you to recognize me. Most people don't. I was a bit younger then." He looked at her directly. "Now, I'll repeat my question. Perhaps you didn't hear me. Who's the teacher?"

Drawing herself up, she said softly, "I'm the teacher."

"Yes, you're the teacher, Miss Green. Remember that," he said. "And now you may go." Rising from his chair he gently took her arm and escorted her to the door.

IVON PREFONTAINE

WINTER NIGHTS

Small children—
Breathlessly wait,
Peer through frosted window
Soak it in.
Heavens ripple—
Lights undulate;
A celebratory fury
An indisputable guide.
This old house speaks;
Nature answers—
Crackles from the heavens
Sweet symphonic sounds.
Earth's floor—
Blanketed in white
Celestial colours shimmer
Captures young eyes.
A vivid winter scene,
A sensual, sensory palette,
Reminds me—
Christ's Mass draws near.

IVON PREFONTAINE

END OF THE WEEK

Turn the soil

Plant the seeds

Offer precious food

Sustaining liquid

Nourish the spirit

A soul grows,

Buoyed—

A light shines

Reveals the path

With each step taken.

Breathe

Barely audible

Life giving

End of week arrives

I wait quietly,

I pause patiently,

I till tenderly,

Turn the soil

Plant the seeds

Take care.

JANE BUEL BRADLEY

FAREWELL TO SPRING

(Godetia deflexa)

This wildflower's four petals
pale pink at the edges,
change to yellow at the center
where bright stamens
frame a white cross.
It opens like a cup
at the top of a long thin
green stem, bearing a procession
of pink, pointed buds.
Every one of these will open
in its turn, giving
a lingering farewell
to the season of promise.
I slow my steps
to see the last of something loved
before meeting the enormous secret
of the future.

PART VIII

ENVY

PHILIP K. DICK

BEYOND THE DOOR

That night at the dinner table he brought it out and set it down beside her plate. Doris stared at it, her hand to her mouth. "My God, what is it?" She looked up at him, bright-eyed.

"Well, open it."

Doris tore the ribbon and paper from the square package with her sharp nails, her bosom rising and falling. Larry stood watching her as she lifted the lid. He lit a cigarette and leaned against the wall.

"A cuckoo clock!" Doris cried. "A real old cuckoo clock like my mother had." She turned the clock over and over. "Just like my mother had, when Pete was still alive." Her eyes sparkled with tears.

"It's made in Germany," Larry said. After a moment he added, "Carl got it for me wholesale. He knows some guy in the clock business. Otherwise I wouldn't have—" He stopped.

Doris made a funny little sound.

"I mean, otherwise I wouldn't have been able to afford it." He scowled. "What's the matter with you? You've got your clock, haven't you? Isn't that what you want?"

Doris sat holding onto the clock, her fingers pressed against the brown wood.

"Well," Larry said, "what's the matter?"

He watched in amazement as she leaped up and ran from the room, still clutching the clock. He shook his head. "Never satisfied. They're all that way. Never get enough."

He sat down at the table and finished his meal.

The cuckoo clock was not very large. It was handmade, however, and there were countless frets on it, little indentations and ornaments scored in the soft wood. Doris sat on the bed drying her eyes and winding the clock. She set the hands by her wristwatch. Presently she carefully moved the hands to two minutes of ten. She carried the clock over to the dresser and propped it up.

Then she sat waiting, her hands twisted together in her lap—waiting for the cuckoo to come out, for the hour to strike.

As she sat she thought about Larry and what he had said. And what she had said, too, for that matter—not that she could be blamed for any of it. After all, she couldn't keep listening to him forever without defending herself; you had to blow your own trumpet in the world.

She touched her handkerchief to her eyes suddenly. Why did he have to say that, about getting it wholesale? Why did he have to spoil it all? If he felt that way he needn't have got it in the first place. She clenched her fists. He was so mean, so damn mean.

But she was glad of the little clock sitting there ticking to itself, with its funny grilled edges and the door. Inside the door was the cuckoo, waiting to come out. Was he listening, his head cocked on one side, listening to hear the clock strike so that he would know to come out?

Did he sleep between hours? Well, she would soon see him: she could ask him. And she would show the clock to Bob. He would love it; Bob loved old things, even old stamps and buttons. He liked to go with her to the stores. Of course, it was a little *awkward*, but Larry had been staying at the office so much, and that helped. If only Larry didn't call up sometimes to—

There was a whirr. The clock shuddered and all at once the door opened. The cuckoo came out, sliding swiftly. He paused and looked around solemnly, scrutinizing her, the room, the furniture.

It was the first time he had seen her, she realized, smiling to herself in pleasure. She stood up, coming toward him shyly. "Go on," she said. "I'm waiting."

The cuckoo opened his bill. He whirred and chirped, quickly, rhythmically. Then, after a moment of contemplation, he retired. And the door snapped shut.

She was delighted. She clapped her hands and spun in a little circle. He was marvelous, perfect! And the way he had looked around, studying her, sizing her up. He liked her; she was certain of it. And she, of course, loved him at once, completely. He was just what she had hoped would come out of the little door.

Doris went to the clock. She bent over the little door, her lips close to the wood. "Do you hear me?" she whispered. "I think you're the most wonderful cuckoo in the world." She paused, embarrassed. "I hope you'll like it here."

Then she went downstairs again, slowly, her head high.

Larry and the cuckoo clock really never got along well from the start. Doris said it was because he didn't wind it right, and it didn't like being only half-wound all the time. Larry turned the job of winding over to her; the cuckoo came out every quarter hour and ran the spring down without remorse, and someone had to be ever after it, winding it up again.

Doris did her best, but she forgot a good deal of the time. Then Larry would throw his newspaper down with an elaborate weary motion and stand up. He would go into the dining room where the clock was mounted on the wall over the fireplace. He would take the clock down and making sure that he had his thumb over the little door, he would wind it up.

"Why do you put your thumb over the door?" Doris asked once.

"You're supposed to." She raised an eyebrow. "Arc you sure? I wonder if it isn't that you don't want him to come out while you're standing so close."

"Why not?"

"Maybe you're afraid of him."

Larry laughed. He put the clock back on the wall and gingerly removed his thumb. When Doris wasn't looking he examined his thumb. There was still a trace of the nick cut out of the soft part of it. Who—or what—had pecked at him?

One Saturday morning, when Larry was down at the office working over some important special accounts, Bob Chambers came to the front porch and rang the bell. Doris was taking a quick shower. She dried herself and slipped into her robe. When she opened the door Bob stepped inside, grinning.

"Hi," he said, looking around.

"It's all right. Larry's at the office."

"Fine." Bob gazed at her slim legs below the hem of the robe. "How nice you look today."

She laughed. "Be careful! Maybe I shouldn't let you in after all."

They looked at one another, half amused half frightened. Presently Bob said, "If you want, I'll—"

"No, for God's sake." She caught hold of his sleeve. "Just get out of the doorway so I can close it. Mrs. Peters across the street, you know."

She closed the door. "And I want to show you something," she said. "You haven't seen it."

He was interested. "An antique? Or what?"

She took his arm, leading him toward the dining room. "You'll love it, Bobby." She stopped, wide-eyed. "I hope you will. You must; you must love it. It means so much to me—*he* means so much."

"He?" Bob frowned. "Who is he?"

Doris laughed. "You're jealous! Come on." A moment later they stood before the clock, looking up at it. "He'll come out in a few minutes. Wait until you see him. I know you two will get along just fine."

"What does Larry think of him?"

"They don't like each other. Sometimes when Larry's here he won't come out. Larry gets mad if he doesn't come out on time. He says—"

"Says what?"

Doris looked down. "He always says he's been robbed, even if he did get it wholesale." She brightened. "But I know he won't come out because he doesn't like Larry. When I'm here alone he comes right out for me, every fifteen minutes, even though he really only has to come out on the hour."

She gazed up at the clock. "He comes out for me because he wants to. We talk; I tell him things. Of course, I'd like to have him upstairs in my room, but it wouldn't be right."

There was the sound of footsteps on the front porch. They looked at each other, horrified.

Larry pushed the front door open, grunting. He set his briefcase down and took off his hat. Then he saw Bob for the first time.

"Chambers. I'll be damned." His eyes narrowed. "What are you doing here?" He came into the dining room. Doris drew her robe about her helplessly, backing away.

"I—" Bob began. "That is, we—" He broke off, glancing at Doris.

Suddenly the clock began to whirr. The cuckoo came rushing out, bursting into sound. Larry moved toward him.

"Shut that din off," he said. He raised his fist toward the clock. The cuckoo snapped into silence and retreated. The door closed. "That's better." Larry studied Doris and Bob, standing mutely together.

"I came over to look at the clock," Bob said. "Doris told me that it's a rare antique and that—"

"Nuts. I bought it myself." Larry walked up to him. "Get out of here." He turned to Doris. "You too. And take that damn clock with you."

He paused, rubbing his chin. "No. Leave the clock here. It's mine; I bought it and paid for it."

In the weeks that followed after Doris left, Larry and the cuckoo clock got along even worse than before. For one thing, the cuckoo stayed inside most of the time, sometimes even at twelve o'clock when he should have been busiest. And if he did come out at all he usually spoke only once or twice, never the correct number of times. And there was a sullen, uncooperative note in his voice, a jarring sound that made Larry uneasy and a little angry.

But he kept the clock wound, because the house was very still and quiet and it got on his nerves not to hear someone running around, talking and dropping things. And even the whirring of a clock sounded good to him.

But he didn't like the cuckoo at all. And sometimes he spoke to him.

"Listen," he said late one night to the closed little door. "I know you can hear me. I ought to give you back to the Germans—back to the Black Forest." He paced back and forth. "I wonder what they're doing now, the two of them. That young punk with his books and his antiques. A man shouldn't be interested in antiques; that's for women."

He set his jaw. "Isn't that right?"

The clock said nothing. Larry walked up in front of it. "Isn't that right?" he demanded. "Don't you have anything to say?"

He looked at the face of the clock. It was almost eleven, just a few seconds before the hour. "All right. I'll wait until eleven. Then I want to hear what you have to say. You've been pretty quiet the last few weeks since she left."

He grinned wryly. "Maybe you don't like it here since she's gone." He scowled. "Well, I paid for you, and you're coming out whether you like it or not. You hear me?"

Eleven o'clock came. Far off, at the end of town, the great tower clock boomed sleepily to itself. But the little door remained shut. Nothing moved. The minute hand passed on and the cuckoo did not stir. He was someplace inside the clock, beyond the door, silent and remote.

"All right, if that's the way you feel," Larry murmured, his lips twisting. "But it isn't fair. It's your job to come out. We all have to do things we don't like."

He went unhappily into the kitchen and opened the great gleaming refrigerator. As he poured himself a drink he thought about the clock.

There was no doubt about it—the cuckoo should come out, Doris or no Doris. He had always liked her, from the very start. They had got along well, the two of them. Probably he liked Bob too—probably he had seen enough of Bob to get to know him. They would be quite happy together, Bob and Doris and the cuckoo.

Larry finished his drink. He opened the drawer at the sink and took out the hammer. He carried it carefully into the dining room. The clock was ticking gently to itself on the wall.

"Look," he said, waving the hammer. "You know what I have here? You know what I'm going to do with it? I'm going to start on you—first." He smiled. "Birds of a feather, that's what you are—the three of you."

The room was silent.

"Are you coming out? Or do I have to come in and get you?"

The clock whirred a little.

"I hear you in there. You've got a lot of talking to do, enough for the last three weeks. As I figure it, you owe me—"

The door opened. The cuckoo came out fast, straight at him. Larry was looking down, his brow wrinkled in thought. He glanced up, and the cuckoo caught him squarely in the eye.

Down he went, hammer and chair and everything, hitting the floor with a tremendous crash. For a moment the cuckoo paused, its small body poised rigidly. Then it went back inside its house. The door snapped tight shut after it.

The man lay on the floor, stretched out grotesquely, his head bent over to one side. Nothing moved or stirred. The room was completely silent, except, of course, for the ticking of the clock.

✤

"I see," Doris said, her face tight. Bob put his arm around her, steadying her.

"Doctor," Bob said, "can I ask you something?"

"Of course," the doctor said.

"Is it very easy to break your neck, falling from so low a chair? It wasn't very far to fall. I wonder if it might not have been an accident. Is there any chance it might have been—"

"Suicide?" the doctor rubbed his jaw. "I never heard of anyone committing suicide that way. It was an accident; I'm positive."

"I don't mean suicide," Bob murmured under his breath, looking up at the clock on the wall. "I meant *something else.*"

But no one heard him.

(Originally Published in *Fantastic Universe*, January 1954)

EDDIE WOODS

GREEN MY ENVY

for Marie Ponsot

Green my envy
sulking in a pool of rage,
wanting for my own ends
Leonardo's brain
and all the wit
that ran with bitter ease
down Pope's scarlet quill.

Let Buddha sit happily
turning his dharma wheel:
lacking Socrates' tongue,
I would rather be the cat
a Zen monk sliced in two.

Did Aquinas laugh
when you first played the Summa
as a pleasant interlude
between lunch and afternoon tea?
Or was it Joyce I saw
tickling your fancy
after another quiet supper
of Finnegan stew?
If only you realized
how much of your hidden mind
my empty luggage carried
around Ulysses' cape.
Not your face
but your unfathomable erudition
launched all those jealous ships
my intellect took to sea.

From beyond the deva worlds
a wise monk shakes his head
while my grey ego sets sail
on a voyage
that can only end tragically.
Seeking perfection,
I may well lose my soul.
Only mindfulness is true.

BARBARA ALFARO

CONFRONTING THE GREEN-EYED MONSTER

There are several possible explanations. Perhaps because I was named Shelley by Lydia (I presume to call her that) who is such a relentless romantic. Perhaps something as simple as a computer error caused the disturbance I am about to describe, it surprises me to say, in an attempt to clarify what occurred. Allow me to tell you a bit about myself and my duration.

I reside with a family named Newton in a house with a view of the river. Lydia is a poet who writes technically imperfect but pleasing sonnets, her husband Edgar is the president of a toy company, and they have a mini-person named Milton. Milton is six years old and apparently all that is required of him is that he wash in back of his ears, and not track dirt into the house. His parents are quite a lovely couple and he is a nice little chap. There is also a miniature mutt mix named Muggie who is neither lovely nor nice.

Like all RA-12 model robots, I was assembled at RoboGenesis. Tall, metallic and intelligent, I have no nose or mouth but do have round green eyes and two coils in place of ears. As is usual in my kind, I have a shiny hairless head, a square torso, two arms, two legs, and large flat feet. I do not know how long I will be permitted to function as there are now so many newer and more efficient robots on the market (RA-13 and other higher generation models have more memory but lower *joie de fonctionnement)*.

There is a No-Disassemble Sanctuary in Utah that accepts defunct robots— but a robot has to have seventeen person references to qualify and I have only served eight people in my duration. It seems inconceivable that I will find nine additional persons to write letters of reference on my behalf at this late point in my duration. And Milton's handwriting is so poor, a letter from him might not be eligible for consideration.

I do not want to be disassembled. I like functioning; I like everything about it. I especially like being here with Lydia, Edgar, and Milton. Birds chirping each morning, mini-persons giggling and playing, the way the river changes from gentle to rapid, sunlight moving here and there, and how the sun and the moon change places each night as if this is an arrangement they had agreed on long ago. And although I am not capable of or programmed for affection, I am comfortable and easy in the presence of the Newtons, whether I am playing the poems of William Blake (a special favorite of mine) for Lydia, enjoying a game of chess with Edgar, or helping Milton with his homework.

The only exception to this platonic perfection is Muggie. According to puppy lore, dogs are affectionate, loyal, and trustworthy. Muggie is surly, selfish, and disobedient but as Lydia, Edgar, and Milton are affectionate, loyal, and trustworthy, they accept his foibles. Actually, "foibles" seems too soft a word as Muggie barks whenever Edgar coughs or sneezes, growls at Milton when he walks by his bowl of dog food, and, quite shockingly, bites lovely Lydia when she tries to remove a burr from his fur. But because of a pair of floppy ears, big brown eyes, and a nose that looks like an oversized gumdrop, this negative behavior is always forgiven. Much has been overlooked because of that big gumdrop nose—because the creature is what persons call "cute." Add to all I have said the fact that Muggie is in the habit of piddling on my feet (thankfully, rustproof).

I am not capable of or programmed for paradox. If I were, I might explore intellectually why a hairy, tailed, barking thing is preferable to a shiny, efficient, quiet one. It does seem a stunning incongruity that Muggie, whose lapses of good behavior so far exceed what is considered acceptable, is every evening petted, cuddled, and snuggled on the living room sofa, while I who have never disobeyed a single directive, am kept in the kitchen along with canned vegetables and coffee pots.

My chief responsibilities are to protect and, if need be, rescue my assigned family members from troubling forces, whether a severe thunderstorm or a dangerous intruder. Sad to say, even in this enlightened day and age, there is still a criminal element in society. But because protector robots now inhabit almost every home, almost every person is safe. I say "almost" because unfortunately only those who can afford to purchase a robot own one. The less fortunate, as is usual in all societies, have to fend for themselves. But I digress.

Not that long ago, I was on the front porch, perusing Proust and pondering the ineffability and uncertainty of all duration when I noticed Muggie chasing a small brown rabbit in the tall grass beside the river. I am not capable of or programmed for empathy but if I were, I would certainly have sided with the rabbit. Suddenly and quite unexpectedly, in the uncontrolled glee of the chase, Muggie lost his balance and fell into the river. The rabbit disappeared in the grass.

I watched as Muggie's furry paws did a quick doggie-paddle but, clearly, the current of the river was too strong for the little canine. Here is the part of the story it troubles me to relate. Though programmed, as aforementioned, to protect and, if need be, rescue—I hesitated. During my temporary lapse, I saw myself playing with Milton, greeting Edgar when he came home from the office, and snuggling (in a metallic, dignified manner) near Lydia while she scratched the back of my coils as the family watched TV. These gentle images were suddenly interrupted by the loud yelping of Muggie still frantically pawing and paddling.

"Why not," I mused, "let nature take its course." Who am I to intrude on the plans Providence may have in store for Muggie? And perhaps, the worst would not occur. Perhaps another family, enjoying an afternoon of boating, would rescue and adopt Muggie as their own. Perhaps...

Suddenly, a force, an inner impulse if you will, impelled me into action. One of my most impressive features is that I am equipped with an emergency inflatable floatation device very like those on huge aircraft, though of course much smaller and slimmer. I initiated this procedure along with its auto pilot option and promptly fell backward and boat-like into the river very near Muggie. He understood the rescue attempt almost immediately and was able to paw and pull his way up onto my chest though his little potbelly proved a momentary encumbrance.

Safely on land, Muggie shook his round little body several times then proceeded to piddle on my right foot though I took this as a sign of his quite understandable nervousness rather than his usual rudeness. I still do not pretend to understand what transpired. I am after all only robotic. Still, since Muggie's almost drowning and my almost...Well, the little fellow does not seem quite as horrid and it is worth noting he has not piddled on my foot in weeks.

PART IX

ENVIRONMENT

CHRIS DAVIDSON

AGAINST

When the world we have grown accustomed to is lost
to desire and depletion, I pray you make your way
through husks of mountains, trees stripped and ossified,
over the rivers' viscous sludge toward a land that bears
colors you see now not yet vanquished. May the machines
have dissolved into spinning parts burrowed into dirt
like animate seeds, transformed in time by the weight of earth—
full now of holes, aerated for no planting, the soil
yielding to u.v given up in soot and slag by our efforts—
into diamonds, packets of light. I pray you see

I didn't know always I was tearing out pieces of the highway
before you; that by miracle ash is returned to fire
in your watch and flames packed back into dry wood;
that clean rain comes to restore to branch the root before,
the shoot above, the kernel concealed no longer
in demineralized dust but dust inhaling the calm breath
of water, pushing out frames of forest unrolling across
ridge and ravine, each tree moving against the pull of gravity,
against vacancy, to reveal like a never-old trick
jewel-like fruit, each without memory against what
consumed it or poison against the hand extending itself
toward it, serving hunger that can be calmed, never curbed.

LUKE SALAZAR

LOST

"Too many choices, America... it's *not healthy.*"
— **George Carlin**

Hunt and gather, hide from cold
need for shelter, need for fire
just to live another day
all we need, all we desire

Then someone invents the plow
soon we farm and soon we build
soon we settle down in place
hunger gone and needs fulfilled

People now have extra time
think of ways life can improve
faster ways to get things done
watch us hustle watch us move

No more sickness no more hate
know our souls will never die
no more danger no more fate
watch our buildings touch the sky

Concrete walls and shopping malls
Snickers, Twix, and pixie sticks
rubber vomit, Tide 'n Comet
SUVs and plastic trees

Stop the madness stop the lies
careful what you make and buy
careful what you throw away
bites us in the ass someday.

JENA ARDELL

THE EMPATHY OF PARANOIA

Hurry kids, come quick! It's time to watch
the world sink!
The dog's sick in the head
and hallucinating again
So grab the solar-powered camera
and the Brita filter gas mask
(makes your water great
while you wait
for air to incinerate!)
The bioluminescent ocean
has been producing radioactive dew
and toxic gumbo is on the menu

The radio stopped playing music years ago
when homicide was on the rise
and the bomb shelter era went Helter Skelter
Yeah, it's fun to see the fish all fry and vegetation die
in this bio-nuclear chemical quagmire
The ash covering trees
resembles the memory of leaves
as its hard to distinguish allies from adversaries
amidst the scam artistry

Cherry blossoms pop as guns are being shot
while mad cows are served with hash browns
to men who get their kicks selling AIDS to local
blood banks in the name of The American Dream
And media photosynthesis has been eradicated
as we are all left frazzled and jaded, dusting soot
from atop our mailbox (when they stop
sending anthrax is when you should worry!)

Politicians become aphasic when continents collide
and we begin singing "The Star Spangled Banner"
in Australia next to Asian eyes
as they desperately try to harmonize
Hooe-Zaaay Cahnn Oooo Z-eeee
at the top of their emphysemic lungs

You know it's time to panic when *The National Enquirer*
is reporting what's closest to the truth
and the message Hallmark sends
is the world's going to end

Hookers were forced from the streets
because they can't compete
standing next to sexy lawyers
who just want some cash fast
as cases of Man vs. Mother Nature fail

Better think of what Beatles song to play
the day you're forced to give your baby away
on the eve they announce heredity
a natural disaster
Karaoke parties will be arranged

by the Disney deranged who brought you
such great films as
Cinderella Does Dallas
and *The Lady, The Other Lady*, and *The Tramp*
(it's how they teach kids about safe sex now!)

Birds have stopped flying in flocks
as we pray around the clock
and are left to wonder
if this is the last dawn
before the ocean comes along
as humanity borderlines
mass insanity

THOM KUDLA

GREEN MEANS GO

Green means go,
but we forgot
to stop at red
before making
the light,
before making
things right.

The catalog said
"Make a difference,"
aiming its sights
at a shirt that read
"Green is the new black."
As if wearing a piece of clothing
made by meek underpaid hands
three worlds apart from us,
from the rare delicate fabrics
that only nature's gracious gifts can provide,
changes the polar bears
drowning in melted ice caps;
or the acid rain crystallized as coal,
blackening our blood
to a thick oil
ready to be fought to the death for;
or the air we breathe
making a daylight run
into a midnight jog
as we gasp from smog,
our lungs clasped shut,

sighing from seeing nothing
but blurred orange men at work
and exhausted overcast skylines.

They say eating organic
is the newest trend.
And yet if they didn't mention
what's trendy

and instead told you
organic food just so happens
to be better for your body
and better for the economy,
you'd chomp on some more
force-fed chicken,
drink down some of that tasty
mutant cow milk,
and consume that plastic-
processed junk you so love.
(I'm sure your heart is bursting
with that kind of love.)
You trendsetter, you.

So I cut myself walking
down the street
in bare feet
the other day.
The light was green.
I had to go.
(Silly me to think
I could go anywhere
without shoes and socks.)
I tried to stop the bleeding,
but it just kept letting itself out,
so I began my trek to the doctor.
I kept going—
upon broken glass bottles,
across jagged concrete,
through rusted wires.
Nothing would stop me
from stopping the bleeding.
By the time I got to the doctor
my feet appeared to have
black and blue
socks and shoes
of their own.
(Oh, I guess I'd mistaken
a swollen bloody mess
for what was once my feet.)
➤

The doc told me
things could've been different—
my feet wouldn't be so black
and bloody and swollen;
I wouldn't have a fever;
and I might even still be able to walk—
had I simply stopped upon getting cut
and asked for someone's help immediately
before going so hastily to his office
to fill out insurance forms and wait,
and wait, and wait,
in a waiting room.
Now I ride around in a wheelchair.
Oh well.
I guess it was a nice walk while it lasted.

LeeAnne McIlroy Langton

OH, GIVE ME A HOME: WATCHING FREE-RANGE CATTLE AT TWILIGHT IN CENTRAL CALIFORNIA

Enjoy these lingering sunsets

Enjoy this fleeting pasture that

Spreads out like a tattered quilt

Upon which those giant, gentle

Sleeping camels of wind-swept hills

Rest their hidden heads

Their fur as warm and wily as yours

Thickets of dried grass weeping in the breeze

Silently mourning the brand that burns your haunches and

The red dot, the bull's-eye

Painted

In the center of your forehead

Announcing your fate

MICHAEL C. KEITH

STEAKS OF WRATH

Joady was no ordinary Angus. Fate had endowed him with the ability to discern human intentions and although that may have seemed a great gift it proved more a horrible burden to the omniscient bovine. He knew he was destined for the slaughterhouse. As is the sad plight of most cattle, he had the misfortune of being born into a world that wished to devour him—one that saw him only as porterhouse, sirloin, T-bone, rib eye, and flank steak. Humans fed him not out of compassion but so they could more sumptuously feast on him. Indeed, nobody took Joady's feelings into account, and he had feelings...*profound* feelings. Foremost among them was a passionate desire to avoid the human dinner table.

The perceptive steer could tell the end was near because the herd had been placed in a holding area and watered and fed at an unusual time. Something was up and he knew what it was. In order to escape his imminent demise, he had to do something that would catch the attention of his soon-to-be executioners...something that would distinguish him from his unknowing and unsuspecting kin. If he could display some unique talent, he might be spared, he thought, and perhaps his being spared might lead to the others being spared as well. Surely they would not kill a cow that could sing, would they?

He moved to where a group of men wearing Stetsons congregated beyond the holding fence and broke into song. First, he performed an aria from Puccini, but he got no response from the humans. Surmising they were not into opera, he then crooned a spirited rendition of "Ring of Fire" by Johnny Cash, but his heartfelt interpretation of the Man in Black's hit only caused a bucket of water to be thrown at him.

"That damn cow's mooing is drivin' me nuts," exclaimed the attacker to his amused associates.

Joady then decided to pull out the stops and perform the Andrew Lloyd Weber songbook, thinking it might result in his salvation—but as soon as he launched into "Music of the Night," another bucket of water was heaved in his direction.

"You won't be bellowing like that much longer, you crazy critter," shouted the unappreciative human.

Clearly, cowpokes had little music appreciation, Joady sadly concluded. So what could he do next to gain their admiration? After a few seconds, he came upon another idea. He would dazzle them with dance. With his rump, he pushed away a few of the curious cows that had gathered near him to make room to do a tango. The "La Giralda" was certain to gain his reprieve he mused while executing a perfect boleo.

As he gracefully pranced around the holding pen, the cowpokes looked at him with alarm for all they saw was a steer teetering from side to side.

"Maybe he got the Mad Cow Disease," said someone in the group, and that prompted Joady to stop his high stepping immediately knowing that cattle with that affliction are quickly put down.

Feeling frustrated and more desperate, Joady searched his mind for another maneuver that might keep him from being butchered. If only they knew me, they surely would not want to kill me, he sighed, and then conceived yet another strategy. He realized people had animals as pets, and he knew they loved those animals. Perhaps he could appeal to that commendable human trait, he thought.

He ambled over to the fence where the men stood. There, he poked his head through the wooden rails and playfully extended his long tongue hoping to be patted. Instead, his snout was whacked with such force by one of the men that it brought tears to his eyes— but even the huge droplets inspired no compassion.

"Scat!! Get out of here, you dumb old bovine!"

It's no use...the world sees no value in us beyond the plate, conceded Joady, withdrawing his head from the fence.

At that moment the door to the slaughterhouse opened and the cattle were formed into a single line and marched toward it. As Joady was prodded into the stunning box, he made a vow to his doomed brethren paraphrasing a soliloquy from his favorite book:

"I'll be all around in the corral. I'll be everywhere—wherever you can look. Wherever there's a fight so cattle can live, I'll be there. Wherever there's a cowhand twisting our tails, I'll be there. I'll be in the way herds moo when they're frightened—I'll be in the way calves bleep when there's no feed in the trough. And when the humans are eating us, I'll be as tough as I can. And at the barbeque, I'll sizzle with contempt over what people do, for I'll be there, too."

Originally published in The Greensilk Journal.

CLINT MARGRAVE

THE ROAD PREVIOUSLY NOT TAKEN

After all the notoriety,
suddenly everyone wanted to take it.
And what started out as a humble dirt path
bending beneath the undergrowth,
had soon been turned into a crowded multi-lane highway with a carpool lane,
the central artery of a bustling strip mall,
equipped with a Target, a Wendy's,
and even an Apple Store.

The other road that had once diverged,
had been bulldozed long ago,
for tract houses and mega churches and a Gymboree,
and the road previously not taken
became rundown from masses of travelers causing traffic jams,
leaving broken clumps of asphalt in the streets,
littering it with Target bags,
Java jackets from the newly built Starbucks,
and sticky plastic spoons
from the Frosty's they ate.

No longer able to maintain it,
and unwilling to raise any unpopular taxes,
the city neglected the road,
to the point of rendering it *untakeable,*
and despite an eleventh-hour attempt
to inject money into making repairs
proved too late to save
the businesses that had folded,
the jobs that had been lost,
the neighborhoods that had been abandoned,
the plywood that had been hammered up
across the windows of all the mega churches.
Too late even to save the Gymboree.

Until ages and ages passed,
and the trees left in the planters
of the abandoned strip mall parking lot
dropped seeds in the cracking asphalt,
and rains washed over everything,
and the winds came,
and new roots began to sprout again,
and the woods grew back,
and after a few more autumns
yellow leaves covered the roofs of all
the abandoned buildings,
and the grasses grew so tall
through the bottom of the rusted shopping carts
that no one could put anything in them,
which made all the difference.

PART X

THE WORLD

BRUCE WEIGL

SONG OF NAPALM
for my wife

After the storm, after the rain stopped pounding,
We stood in the doorway watching horses
Walk off lazily across the pasture's hill.
We stared through the black screen,
Our vision altered by the distance
So I thought I saw a mist
Kicked up around their hooves when they faded
Like cut-out horses
Away from us.
The grass was never more blue in that light, more
Scarlet; beyond the pasture
Trees scraped their voices into the wind, branches
Crisscrossed the sky like barbed wire
But you said they were only branches.

Okay. The storm stopped pounding.
I am trying to say this straight: for once
I was sane enough to pause and breathe
Outside my wild plans and after the hard rain
I turned my back on the old curses. I believed
They swung finally away from me…

But still the branches are wire
And thunder is the pounding mortar,
Still I close my eyes and see the girl
Running from her village, napalm
Stuck to her dress like jelly,
Her hands reaching for the no one
Who waits in waves of heat before her.

So I can keep on living,
So I can stay here beside you,
I try to imagine she runs down the road and wings
Beat inside her until she rises
Above the stinking jungle and her pain
Eases, and your pain, and mine.
➤

But the lie swings back again.
The lie works only as long as it takes to speak
And the girl runs only as far
As the napalm allows
Until her burning tendons and crackling
Muscles draw her up
into that final position

Burning bodies so perfectly assume. Nothing
Can change that; she is burned behind my eyes
And not your good love and not the rain-swept air
And not the jungle green
Pasture unfolding before us can deny it.

GERALD LOCKLIN

NO GREEN BERLIN

In my memory of a few days in Berlin,
There is no green.
A Molecule Man stands tall
In the River Spree, but molecules are not
Holes; real men eschew high heels;
And neither polio not panzer divisions
Assault us in our time.

Every metropolis has its Hauptbahnhof,
Its stately bustling Central Station,
But beautiful buildings cannot be held
Responsible for the uses to which they are put.

Berlin beckons us to the self-igniting flame
Of the Crystal Cupola on the New Reichstag,
Like the bare, skeletal gams of Marlene Dietrich.

Potsdamer Platz is not Potsdam,
(Though Potsdam isn't either).
The trenchant faces of its trilogy of buildings
Are a post-human Carnival of Triangulating Circuitries:
You enter the matrix and emerge a lesser person.

The Bode Museum on Museum Island
Bears witness to Postmodern Capitals as
Museums of Themselves.

The poster of a Russian Soldier at Checkpoint Charlie:
So young, so young, to be the cruel captain of Purgation.

The Twin Towers and identical ticket booths
Of Olympic Stadium exhibit a fashionable functionality.
Only the paving stones of the parking lots
Are irregularly cracked, perhaps by Der Fuhrer's Rage
For and against the future Jesse Owens augured.

The Christmas Market at the
Kaiser Wilhelm Memorial Church:
Who would ever want to forget
Kaiser Bill, Kaiser Billie?

➤

New buildings built within the ruins of Old:
As with Coventry and Cordoba, it can be a
Great idea, but the New Synagogue on
Oranienburger Strasse may present
A slightly too inviting target.

Oh My God: between the small reflecting pool
And the Red Town Hall and Television Tower
I can't deny that I discern a minimal strip of lawn.
I bet it has been planted in the last ten years, which have
Seen Germany become the creditor of the European Union.
Maybe even in honor of Greenback Dollars,
And Daddy Warbucks. But how rich is any creditor
If his debtors will never afford to pay him back?

Walking to the Cultural Center constructed from
A brewery in the former East Berlin, I note the
Cafés full of aspiring writers, artists, intellectuals—
Most, I am told, on the dole—also the aging pensioners
In their aging apartment buildings, desecrated with
Left-wing graffiti. I am patronizingly assured
The audience is fluent beyond belief in English, but
That proves not to extend to my vernacular ironies,
Sarcasms, and ambiguities. I spend most of my mic-time
Singing Sinatra and Streisand, tap-dancing, and soaring
Ceilingward (well, a few inches anyway) like
The World's Oldest Male Peter Pan, the oldest
Female being Cathy Rigby.

I've forgotten what or how many victories are
Celebrated by the Victory Column. Those of
Vercingetorix? Wasn't he Swiss? The trees and
Winged Victory loom black against the torrid sky.

Of course there is a famous zoo, a famous deer park:
Maybe the animals are painted green. Maybe they are
Cannons in camouflage. I do not visit them.
I don't sample the renowned nightlife decadence,
Because I'm watching over my daughter,

Less than a year after 9/11, who will commence
The Turning Point of Law School in the fall.
She is invisibly and invariably green of heart
And always will be. Others may be green with envy,
Who need not be, who have earned their own
Inviolable laurels and inestimable love.

What have I learned from Berlin? That
Fascism and Communism and Unrestrained
Capitalism all combat the vernal culmination
Of renewal, suck the green from memory.
Your memories of Berlin may be more colorful;
My mental palate may have been in atrophy.
And of all cities it's the one I most long to
Revisit, for a longer stay, alone, perhaps,
To quaff my fix of Weimar Blue Angelic,
And then go to hell.

(Previously unpublished. Written January 2013.)

Brooke Nia

$5,000 A WELL

*Unsafe water and lack of basic sanitation cause 80% of diseases, kill-
ing more people each year than all forms of violence, including war.
It costs $5,000 to build a freshwater well, which provides hundreds of
people with access to clean, safe water for decades. Charitywater.org*

She knows the road's iron-red
hue too well, traces death with her long
toe like a child's painting,
Eight-year-old callous
chronicles earth's course grain.

Mile nine, she dips her yellow pail
into a mosquito-littered puddle,
collects the green liquid
she will use to poison her family.

Doubled over, her father cannot
gather sorghum to feed his sons,
sell grain at the market
where babies are bottle-fed salmonella
as villagers grow tumors like cantaloupe.

Dysentery's hollow quiver digests stomach,
sour wince of lower bowel.

She invents laughing children
in plateau shadows
who vanish suddenly as
young cousins disappear from
her *ghotiya's* thick, mud walls.

She knows loss like an alphabet
she will never learn,
mothers' parched graves
familiar as Sahara horizon.

She studies cracks in stone
like contours of her father's brow;
miles scissor flesh, a travel log
pummeled in ancient young skin,
cheeks rouged with sienna dust,
mouth split like Sudan's fractured canyons.

On her head, she carries the disease,

now half her weight,
neck twisted like Marula root,
curved by age she will never reach.

JAMES JOYCE

DUBLINERS
GREEN EXCERPTS

It may have been these constant showers of snuff which gave his ancient priestly garments their green faded look for the red handkerchief, blackened, as it always was, with the snuff stains of a week, with which he tried to brush away the fallen grains, was quite inefficacious.

All the branches of the tall trees which lined the mall were gay with little light green leaves and the sunlight slanted through them on to the water. The granite stone of the bridge was beginning to be warm and I began to pat it with my hands in time to an air in my head. I was very happy.

I saw a man approaching from the far end of the field. I watched him lazily as I chewed one of those green stems on which girls tell fortunes. He came along by the bank slowly. He walked with one hand upon his hip and in the other hand he held a stick with which he tapped the turf lightly. He was shabbily dressed in a suit of greenish-black and wore what we used to call a jerry hat with a high crown. He seemed to be fairly old for his moustache was ashen-grey. When he passed at our feet he glanced up at us quickly and then continued his way.

Polly was a slim girl of nineteen; she had light soft hair and a small full mouth. Her eyes, which were grey with a shade of green through them, had a habit of glancing upwards when she spoke with anyone, which made her look like a little perverse madonna.

The light and noise of the bar held him at the doorways for a few moments. He looked about him, but his sight was confused by the shining of many red and green wine-glasses The bar seemed to him to be full of people and he felt that the people were observing him curiously. He glanced quickly to right and left (frowning slightly to make his errand appear serious), but when his sight cleared a little he saw that nobody had turned to look at him: and there, sure enough, was Ignatius

Gallaher leaning with his back against the counter and his feet planted far apart.

♣

There was a great deal of laughing and joking during the meal. Lizzie Fleming said Maria was sure to get the ring and, though Fleming had said that for so many Hallow Eves, Maria had to laugh and say she didn't want any ring or man either; and when she laughed her greygreen eyes sparkled with disappointed shyness and the tip of her nose nearly met the tip of her chin. Then Ginger Mooney lifted her mug of tea and proposed Maria's health while all the other women clattered with their mugs on the table, and said she was sorry she hadn't a sup of porter to drink it in. And Maria laughed again till the tip of her nose nearly met the tip of her chin and till her minute body nearly shook itself asunder because she knew that Mooney meant well though, of course, she had the notions of a common woman.

♣

The gentlemen were all well dressed and orderly. The light of the lamps of the church fell upon an assembly of black clothes and white collars, relieved here and there by tweeds, on dark mottled pillars of green marble and on lugubrious canvases. The gentlemen sat in the benches, having hitched their trousers slightly above their knees and laid their hats in security. They sat well back and gazed formally at the distant speck of red light which was suspended before the high altar.

♣

A fat brown goose lay at one end of the table and at the other end, on a bed of creased paper strewn with sprigs of parsley, lay a great ham, stripped of its outer skin and peppered over with crust crumbs, a neat paper frill round its shin and beside this was a round of spiced beef.

Between these rival ends ran parallel lines of side-dishes: two little minsters of jelly, red and yellow; a shallow dish full of blocks of blancmange and red jam, a large green leaf-shaped dish with a stalk-shaped handle, on which lay bunches of purple raisins and peeled almonds, a companion dish on which lay a solid rectangle of Smyrna figs, a dish of custard topped with grated nutmeg, a small bowl full of chocolates and sweets wrapped in gold and silver papers and a glass vase in which stood some tall celery stalks. In the centre of the table there stood, as sentries to a fruit stand which upheld a pyramid of oranges and American apples, two squat old-fashioned decanters of cut glass, one containing port and the other dark sherry. On the closed square piano a pudding in a huge yellow dish lay in waiting and behind it were three squads of bottles of stout and ale and minerals, drawn up according to the colours of their uniforms, the first two black, with brown and red labels, the third and smallest squad white, with transverse green sashes.

Gabriel took his seat boldly at the head of the table and, having looked to the edge of the carver, plunged his fork firmly into the goose. He felt quite at ease now for he was an expert carver and liked nothing better than to find himself at the head of a well-laden table.

At that moment the hall door was opened and Mr. Browne came in from the doorstep, laughing as if his heart would break. He was dressed in a long green overcoat with mock astrakhan cuffs and collar and wore on his head an oval fur cap. He pointed down the snow-covered quay from where the sound of shrill prolonged whistling was borne in.

"Teddy will have all the cabs in Dublin out," he said.

CLIFTON SNIDER

ADIEU À HOSPITAAL

The gray-haired doctor
with quadrasyllabic name
has said I can leave
in time to catch my flight.

My Flemish friend
totes my bags,
packs me tight
into his car.

The train is late &
schoolboys wait,
repeating their lessons,
playing cards, smoking.

The cold gray day
is gorgeous,
I love it:
Zeus, Ganymede.

Guy goes to check
why the "wagons"
do not come & in the act
they do. We

cannot say good-bye
but wave.
I drag my bags into
the right car,

the one that is secure:
Bruges to Frankfurt.
Yogurt never tasted
so good as now.

Europe never breathed
so green, never
was so wet, never boasted
a brighter rainbow.

> —from *Moonman: New and Selected Poems*
> (World Parade Books, 2012)

PART XI

LOVE & MARRIAGE

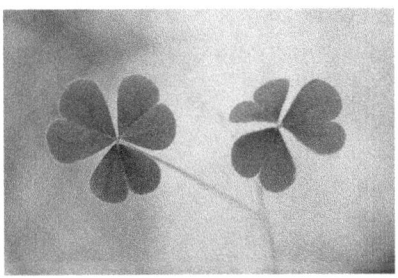

BARBARA EKNOIAN

THE GREEN CROFT

I'm sixteen working at The Green Croft,
a family inn, green-shuttered,
four stories high
right on Lake Hopatcong.
On the porch every night after supper,
my friends and I rock back and forth
in our chairs like old grannies
while the rich kids
whiz by in their speedboats.
Across the lake, the Bon Air Lodge
is lit up like an electric power plant.
We hear music from their band
and wish we were older to venture
across the River Styx Bridge
to attend their big Labor Day bash.
On our porch, the ancient jukebox
houses only one modern song.
I play Elvis's
"I want you, I need you, I love you,"
over and over
pining for a boy back home.

One night, Charlie, a guest who looks
like a forty-year-old bookworm,
sits at the upright piano playing,
"A Whole Lot of Shaking Going On"
 as good as Jerry Lee Lewis.
Guests push the Ping-Pong table aside,
start to rock 'n' roll.
Peter the waiter tries to pull me up
to Lindy, but I'm too shy and say no.
He grabs Kathy, the waitress,
flips her around like the "Swing Kids."
I sit there and feel the floorboards
vibrating beneath me
as Charlie bangs the piano
and pumps the foot pedal below.

BROOKE NIA

THANKFUL

In Wranglers, heels and a turquoise
bra, I patina lips pink, room swollen
with thick, gold light. You sit
cross-legged, strumming your '78 Guild.

My notes coil in yours like mollusks
fold diaphanous bodies in shell.

On iceplant in your backyard
we ponder God, Hugh Heffner
our fathers' coronaries till 5am
watching lattice grate moonlight
in fat slices, blister bougainvilleas
to papery white embers.

We tear melaleuca bark into cave
paintings, cartwheel on wet grass
in front of the funeral home on 19th,
make my grandmother's Wiener Schnitzel
recipe from scratch; I squirm while
you tenderize pork, tease me
holding one side of my waist
with your free hand.

Under a streetlamp on Olive Bridge
you pull the car over, put on your hazards
open my door. Red and white streak by
like necklaces, horns plummet.
You twirl me, black strapless dress
blossoms around my knees.
We dance on sidewalk's orange hue
La Cañada's eyes glistening.

Dreaming naked, you are my bedding
braid my body like satin, chant my name
in your sleep. I scale your torso mornings
before dew cowers to sun,
ash blonde hair suspended around faces like
curtains, my hipbones exhume your abs.
Prone beneath me in dawn's
bleeding light, you ask
What if we had a family?

We pray over breakfast
2 eggs, toast, a mango smoothie
I'm so thankful.
I don't know you'll leave
the next day.

BROOKE NIA

SOPELANA

Wednesday afternoon
I googled the cliff where
we first kissed in Spain.

I could see wind
even in the still image
and the bluffs were empty.

I dragged my mouse across
vacant city, featureless buildings
scanning the landscape for feelings
I lost on Lehendakari Aguirre
Sarriko, Moyua.
San Inazio—
the metro stop where you left
without kissing me.

I don't miss hills of Gipuzkoa
where I learned the word green
or forceful *sílabos castellanos*
and *ceceos,* punctuated with
aboriginal *x's* and *k's* of Euskara,
each word a linguistic artifact
in the excavation of sound.

I don't miss whitewashed houses
of Getxo, green and red flags raised
like Batasuna fists, salted *bacalao* hanging
from windowsills in the houses of fishermen
whose rowboats stud water like earrings.

Nor wine from La Rioja
puckered like blood oranges
Sergio's love notes
made of *amaneceres*
steeples of Estefania's laughter
or silver reflections of Guggenheim's
flowery edges in Río Nervión.

How do I miss your red eyes
when I left, my tears
and the pretense you didn't care?

TATE SWINDELL

PHOTOSYNTHETIC

For once in the mirror
I saw leaves
            of green

Burnt brown branches
                        Some thriving   Some dying
Frayed at the edges
                    T o o   f a r   from the roots
Dehydrated
Wanting

Pen to paper
Brush to canvas
Natural
        strokes
                of
                    fingers
                        on
                            keys

Your eyes
A conduit
Remind me to breathe

The vastness inside
Canyons
            Craters
                    Cavities

My heart
No longer arable
Engulfed by your
Tourniquet of love

JOE HAKIM

MIND THE GAP

It's unnatural,
all of us crammed in
like last minute revision.

As I hurtle towards my destination,
I'm surrounded by
people with headphones stuffed
into their ears to block
out the noise,
all staring at a fixed point
on the floor
trying not to meet anyone's gaze;
desperately trying not to acknowledge
one another,
desperately trying to shut the world
out.
All of these people trying to be
invisible.

It's ridiculous,
We
Are
Ridiculous,

and I have to fight the urge
to laugh in everyone's face.
And as I try to stifle a grin,
I look up
and I see her.

I see her
arms folded across a sea-green top
I see her
legs emerge from her skirt
like a run of good luck.

And she sees me.
She looks me in the eye
and she sees me
smiling
and she smiles back

and for a moment
we connect,
both sensing the absurdity
of the situation,
sharing it like a private joke.
And in that moment
I want her
so much –
and in that moment
I would give anything
in the world
to be near her,

because she isn't afraid
to exist,
and her smile reminds me that
I exist.

As I approach my stop
I get up and take a final look
at her
before I leave,
let her crystallise
in my mind
and become a memory,
a reminder that
in the space within the gaps
between us all

there's still enough room
for a little bit of hope.

AL BASILE

NEW WORLDS REWRITTEN

No, my love, we didn't invent spring.
But as earth puts up shoots, and trees awaken
from winter dreams to find our love alive,
they are reminded what the spring is for.

My heart's bread, no—I never said that I
invented love. But as ours, which began
on peaks and ended in the sky, prepares
to fall on peaks again; as patiently
our children wait outside of time, until
they can begin to wait in it for their
own tender hands and tiny beating hearts,

each particle of joy we'll have together
swarms to you from the future in a rush,
renumbers your heart bit by bit, creates
another beating in its place, one that
will tell you soon that you have loved me always.

Your eyes widen and soften, and I hear
the bells that ring out at the ends of wars.
I smell dinner in your touch. Our bodies
weave together, your face blooms into
its joy, and we become what those explorers
who discovered new worlds thought they'd found.

PHILIP VERMAAS

THE PASSING STRANGER

A grey man was passing through a leafy green park.

"Pssst!" he heard from a flowerbed and curiously went over.

"Yes?" enquired the man.

A yellow flower said to him, "Please take me home. I'm a sad yellow flower who wants to leave the green park, to experience something in life, to rise above my peers. In return I will give you beauty. I'll be my most beautiful for you.

"No!" said the man emphatically.

"Why?" asked the flower mournfully.

"I'll tell you," he said and told the flower a story…

A pink man saw a yellow flower. How beautiful, he thought, and marveled at the universe.

But the flower spoke to him. "Take me home," it said.

"I couldn't do that," said the man. "I marvel at the universe because it possesses me. Me who marvels, not me who possesses."

"Please," begged the flower. "I'm not appreciated here, not as I am, amongst many. Not everyone marvels at my beauty, silly man."

"But," pleaded the man, "if I were to pluck you, you would certainly die and I'd have killed something I loved."

"Well," said the flower, strangely happy, "don't pluck me, uproot, uproot, transplant me, as they say, and I will live my natural course."

"No!" frowned the man. "I couldn't deprive the people who would stop and marvel at you. I don't wish to own your beauty."

"I've already told you," said the flower, "no one takes the time to appreciate one yellow flower of a multitude. It is my very simplicity that begets much of my beauty. Look around, look how many there are like me. I'm common and won't be missed. But if you take me I will rise above my fellow flowers, whose beauty goes overlooked everyday."

The man looked upon the beautiful flower. To him it was already distinguished, peerless, but he could find no fault with the flower's reasoning. So, carefully, he dug it out at the root and, just as carefully, carried it home. At home, he found the flower an old grey cake tin and punched drainage holes through the bottom.

"There you are, my flower," he said. "Maybe you are right. Maybe you will help me marvel at the universe a little each day."

"I think we'll be very happy together," said the flower.

The next day, the man went to his living room to see the flower, to see if he really would be able to marvel at the universe. The flower was just waking and the man marveled at the universe.

"You were right about everything, flower," said the man. "I love you, flower."

"I thank you for loving me, dear man," said the flower sleepily.

Everything went well. Every morning, the man would marvel at the universe and tell the flower he loved it. The flower's reply was always the same: "I thank you for loving me, dear man."

Then, one day, the man found the flower looking sad and unwell. It was wilting.

"What's wrong?" asked the man.

The flower spoke softly. "I'm dying," said the flower.

"Don't do that, dear flower. Tell me what more I can do? I've given you water and sunlight and, above all, I've given you love."

The flower cried. "There is nothing to do but to let me die."

"I've got it!' exclaimed the man. "I'll hurry you back to your spot in the leafy green park. You grew well there."

"It's no use," cried the flower, but the man took no notice. He grabbed the tin and set off for the park.

Soon the man had brought the dying flower back to its surrounding, to its place in the flower bed.

The flower still cried. "It's no use. It's too late."

"I can't believe it," said the man as he sat next to the flower. He too began to cry. "You were a fool to have asked me to take you away. Look, now you're dying."

"No," whispered the flower, "you're the fool. If you cry when a flower dies how are you going to cope with the rest of your life?"

"I'm a man," he said, "it's man's nature to cry when something he loves dies."

"Do you see, flower?" said the man, having finished his story. "I'm wiser for knowing that story."

"I see," said the flower, "but surely if you are wiser for knowing that story then you'll not cry when I die."

"That's where you are wrong. It's my nature to cry when things I love die. Now I just know to avoid it."

"You are evolved," said the flower. "'If only I had something other than my beauty with which to tempt you, then you might take me home."

"But?" asked the man seriously. "Why would you want to leave if you knew you were going to die?"

The flower smiled. "Because I know something you don't."

"Yes?" asked the man.

"I know that you're the man in your story."

"True," said the man. "How do you know that?"

"Because," smiled the flower, "because I'm that flower. So, you see, I did not die and so have nothing to fear."

"Tough," said the man, "my lesson is learnt. I'm glad you lived but you were only lucky. So, dear flower, you see that I learn anyway. I am evolved and have evolved. I am man, that's my nature."

The flower conceded. "I cannot fault you. Goodbye, passing stranger."

That very day, the flower died.

HENRY VIII OF ENGLAND

GREEN GROWETH THE HOLLY

Green groweth the holly,
So doth the ivy.
Though winter blasts blow never so high,
Green groweth the holly.
As the holly groweth green
And never changeth hue,
So I am, ever hath been,
Unto my lady true.
As the holly groweth green
With ivy all alone
When flowers cannot be seen
And greenwood leaves be gone,

Now unto my lady
Promise to her I make,
From all other only
To her I me betake.

Adieu, mine own lady,
Adieu, my special
Who hath my heart truly
Be sure, and ever shall.

TRADITIONAL[*]

GREENSLEEVES (Excerpts)

Alas, my love, you do me wrong,
To cast me off discourteously.
For I have loved you well and long,
Delighting in your company.

Greensleeves was all my joy
Greensleeves was my delight,
Greensleeves was my heart of gold,
And who but my lady greensleeves.

My men were clothed all in green,
And they did ever wait on thee;
All this was gallant to be seen,
And yet thou wouldst not love me.

Ah, Greensleeves, now farewell, adieu,
To God I pray to prosper thee,
For I am still thy lover true,
Come once again and love me.

---

[*] Often attributed, in error, to Henry VIII.

PAMELA MILLER WOOD

OXIDATIVE SPIRIT

My dear Life…why do you taunt me so?

You can be so sweet at times—I want to kiss you all over

Then—as I begin to trust—you throw a sucker-punch to the heart

You can be so damn cruel—I hate you—and wish you were dead

You abuse, confuse, entertain, and excite—igniting passion—keeping
    me alive with foolish anticipation

Like the lonely heart sitting too long in the dimly lit booth for two—
    refusing to believe she's been

forsaken—you call again asking for another chance

Why do I continue to believe that shiny brass ring—which long ago
    turned green—is still within reach?

Oh, Life—you rascally bastard—I still find you irresistible—despite
    your constant betrayal with every passing year…

KENDALL STEINLE

CORNFIELDS REVISITED

it started here,
it ended here,

we'll call that coming "full circle."

he squeezed her hand and said, you're not the first,

but you're the first that's even come close to counting.
pause.

and if love was real, it would be this.

the corn shrilled with laughter.

a tear dropped and cracked the ground wide open

and the weeds came pouring out like lava,

the salt from shattered hope

budding the little green noisome stragglers of the plant world.

he left.
she stayed.
some stalks are still there, but dead.
and the weeds?

well,

they're doing just fine.

KENDALL STEINLE

LIMBS

I suppose it's a lack of intuition,
a missing link or two on the chain of cognition.
Everyone else is able to tell which way each limb is twisting,
the sounds of sockets popping so easily discernible,
and there I am, waking up in the middle of the night,
frightened by the unfamiliar auditory interruption.

I asked you once: *How did you know?*
You told me once: *I didn't. I just had a hunch. I just went out on a
limb.*

So I'll sit there.
In that chair. In my driveway. In the middle of Monroe Falls.
I'll scan all the vegetation around me,
both the living and breathing green and the dead and gaunt brown,
but I must be way, way off: *Where the hell is that tree?*

You went out on a limb and you got what you wanted, so
I need to find that tree: within the bark and gum of that stick of wood
    I shall find the demeanor that I exhibit, and I have to kill it.
(I have to find who I am and then destroy me.)

Maybe arsonists are just trying to find themselves?
Maybe forest fires are just brilliant epiphanies?

You traced every inch of my limbs with yours,
and I, for the life of me, cannot find that tree.

GAIA HOLMES

THE MAN WHO DRIPPED DIGITALIS

He could charm the poison out of foxgloves
and used his skills to quicken my pulse.
I wondered what he fed on, frayed liturgies
and the secret dreams of women,
toxic spores translated into messages
of lust, slivers of the dank March sky
rolled up like pickled herring.
I never knew. He always skimmed me,
left me hooked on some potent pollen,
some sacrificial line,
some cold gap between sentiments.

His fingers were like cathedrals,
too big to untie my delicate knots
yet he knew me inside out like he knew
the names of flowers and bats and clouds,
like he knew how to throw daggers
without skewering the soul.
He could sniff out creeping wolfmen
and crack their backbones with a lazy wink,
worked my fingers to his throat
like a snakecharmer,
made me slide and arch with his singing breath.
After we'd loved and I was doped up on glow
he laid wet silver on my eyelids
believing it would bring him luck.

From *Lifting The Piano With One Hand*
(Comma Press, Spring 2013)

MERRILL FARNSWORTH

LABYRINTH

Only once. One shot. One chance.
The one. One of many twisting and
turning on the labyrinth toward
the center. A unique intersection of time
and space shapes each journey into
a story only one life can tell.
He won't forgive. She can't forget.
Some stories are told in one breath,
others unfold in slow, hesitant steps.
Some contemplate, others evaporate.
He thinks only of his next meal.
She updates her Facebook status.
Some walk in shadow on a rainy day,
others see their shadow and know
they are not alone. Some walk labyrinths
of smooth stone, one traveler feels the
sharp crunch of gravel under worn boots,
a reluctant pilgrim is soothed by the
fragrance of fresh-cut grass giving
sweet sway under bare feet.
His silence is cold. She won't shut up.
Just when it seems each sojourner is
closing in on the final destination
the path leads back to where it
begins, or so it seems. Some sense
sacred geometry in the journey,
others simply trudge on in a series of steps
towards or away from their one true story.
Few understand the labyrinth within the labyrinth
or the dream within the dream that is nothing but real.
He can defeat monsters. She can fly upside down.
We dance in fire and walk on water. Only once.

MERRILL FARNSWORTH

MOST DAYS

When she's in the mood
for solitude
she can make a cat lonely
and a dog, if she had one, well
he might as well go next door
for his pat on the head.
It's not that she's mean
or cold, or uncaring,
it's just that she's her.
Stick around and she'll serve
sunshine for breakfast then
wrap herself around you
like there's no tomorrow,
arms, legs and elbows entwine
until the two of you are a tangle
of ivy, ash and evergreen.
When you awake you might find her
nestled down deep in the cradle
of a crescent moon fast asleep,
or wandering canyons in Wyoming
having hammered No Trespassing signs
on all four corners of the state.
If you love her you must be
brave enough, or foolish enough
to take a chance on her. She really,
really hopes you will. Most days.

JOAN JOBE SMITH

CHICAGO

Driving my green '72 Dodge four-door with
green upholstery: a perfect getaway car for a
spy in a broccoli forest, I went to see my
lover for nine years every weekend 42 miles
away in L.A. and listened to my Sinatra tape
as I sped upon the freeways through the grand
canyon of all those Goliath-shouldered skyscrapers
and when Frank sang "Chicago," I'd sing along
"My kind of town LOS ANGELES IS" because I
couldn't wait to see my lover even though he
didn't love me, wouldn't take me to Chicago
where I wanted to go more than Paris or Rome
Chicago where he went all the time to see his
folks and I couldn't go because he was ashamed
of me because I was married and wanted me
to stay that way and one day while I sang along
with Sinatra singing "Chicago," right around that
freeway mesa in downtown L.A. where everyone's
deciding where he's going: Pasadena, Ventura,
Santa Monica, Bakersfield, a car older than mine
ahead of me had a blowout and its wheel rubber
black exploded all the way around and came straight
at me and my Dodge and I swerved into the fast lane
to miss it and found a miracle in the eye of the
hurry-cane: no pickup towing a speedboat, no
oil tanker, no RV loaded with kids and bicycles
just me and my green '72 Dodge and Frank Sinatra
and Chicago: strange, lucky angels hightailing it
onto the Hollywood Freeway to the Echo Park off-ramp
to Sunset Boulevard and left onto Lucile to my lover's
tiny garage-converted pad and our wows and what-ifs.
Later, after I divorced my husband and my lover got
cold feet and pushed me off the 100th story of a
heartbreak hotel, I landed into the arms of a
tall, dark, handsome poet and my ex-lover
went to Chicago with someone else.

FRED VOSS

SIR GAWAIN TAKES OUT THE TRASH

Frank with Jane
and home from the grueling steel-bending-and-chewing machine shop Friday night
wants to celebrate his victory over yet another manhood-testing
week of work
and opens *Sir Gawain and the Green Knight*
reading it aloud to Jane
as a fair lady of the castle tells Sir Gawain,
"You are known as the noblest knight of your age,"
and Frank tells Jane how important courtesy was to Sir Gawain.
"Oh," Jane says,
"You mean like the way you
let the door slam in my face when we're going into a restaurant…"
Frank frowns
but continues to read aloud as Sir Gawain
puts on his armor and helmet and picks up his sword with gold-gilded hilt
and mounts his noble horse Gringolet.
"Ah," says Jane,
"Just the way you put on your jeans and T-shirt and steel-toed boots and pick up
your lunch pail and brave freeway traffic jams
driving to work in your Toyota…"
and Frank reads on and Sir Gawain leaves the castle
to ride through the medieval English woods where wild boar and wolves roam
to find the Green Chapel
in the wild rocky valley and face the fearsome Green Knight
and test
his New Year's Eve oath by letting the Green Knight strike him a blow
across his neck with a might axe.
"Oh, Jane says
"Well, I cut up some stinky fish today.
On your way to the Green Chapel,
could you please take out the trash?"
Frank rises nobly
and closes *Sir Gawain and the Green Knight*
and goes into the kitchen and grabs the trash and heads out their apartment
door
and treks down into the wild rocky medieval English valley
of the cracked asphalt Long Beach alley full of thrown-out mattresses
and faces down the terror of the black trash dumpster
the way Sir Gawain laid his neck under the Green Knight's axe
and throws out the stinky fish
and quotes the ending to *Sir Gawain and the Green Knight:*
➤

"Now that man who wore a crown of thorns
he brings us to his bliss! Amen,"
brushing off his hands
triumphant
in his trash can quest
as the Green Knight tells him,
"You are the most faultless man
that ever walked the earth."

DANIEL MCGINN

MORNINGS AT OUR HOUSE

Maybe it was early in the day. I must have been thinking about the moon, how it sometimes lingers well into the morning. We have nights like that sometimes, nights when moons recede like hairlines, nights that never set. Our alarms refuse to go off. Every bird is just a meadowlark and come what will the moon refuses to fall from the sky. It leaves us hanging.

There was nothing left to do but rub Lori's back. That was how I wanted it that fine day when we laid down in green grass, not an itch to scratch, my eyes closed, just the feel of her skin against my hand. I was holding the most colorful crayon box of feelings. I had chosen her shoulder and started drawing lazy circles when I felt the urge to open the corner of one eye and peek over her side.

There was nothing there. The grass blurred as it spread out across my field of vision and took a right angle climb. A smooth green wall, that is what I saw, but there was nothing there, not yet.

We must be facing to the east I said to myself as my hand rode the slide and splashed into the blue pool of Lori's swayback. I dove in with my eyes closed. I began making wings with my rippling fingers.

I knew if I looked again there might be booths and tents and people who looked like farmers milling around us. I opened my eyes and sure enough, there they were. A meek man in overalls was leaning over us holding a black and white ceramic cow with a basket handle. At that moment that cow was all he cared about. He inquired concerning the nearest cash register, there wasn't one. I stalled for time and dreamed one up. I pointed him to the left. He left. He stood in a back corner of my mind where the green wall rose and blurred. He quietly waited for the cashier to arrive.

I slipped my hand back down into the blue pool of Lori's back and I held my breath. The world was mute for a moment. Lori fluttered up her eyelids. We grew wings. We felt like a couple of birds. We flew away.

PART XII

FAMILY

LeeAnne McIlroy Langton

THE RAINBOW'S END

Years from now
Your grandchildren will
See what you dream of
This last night of your hunger
During the passage from Belfast
Across a sea of storms and slave bones:
Food
In abundance—
Phosphorescent corn bursting from husks,
Blood-colored tomatoes bouncing out of crates
Like giant rubber balls,
Pistachios and almonds raining silently from leafy boughs,
Lettuce heads blossoming open like gardenias,
Grapefruits the size of cannonballs
And oranges as sweet as your grandmother's final tears
Rolling out of the trees
Swimming into the mouth of the Delta
Washed down with the precious nectar of
The California Aqueduct.
Years from now your granddaughter will
Feel that enchanted sense of déjà vu
And you will try to explain to her
(Through the whispers in the grass)
That she is living the vision of the dream you had
The last night on that ship
When you had
Nothing in your stomach
Except a moldy crust of bread
And nothing in your heart
Except the tiniest seeds
Of hope

LORI McGINN

LIGHT

#1
Dew on the morning flower
Moonlight falling on the fallen rose

What a whispering sorrow
What a blanket of feathers we lie in

These years are not forever green
These leaves loose their song, swallowed in a whimper

I wear your cloak, pretend they are elvin arms
You carry a white stone, with my name on it

#2
My desire to be buried is forgotten
Your little pink hat is the attitude you wear

What a flower you are
What a silken doll

These years in my grandchildren's arms
These grape-leaved arbors we run and laugh in

I haven't figured out what color I am dreaming
I don't know the season of my last breath

#3
Heaven bows its wings
I bow down in the gold of you

In our new language
I have no more words

MARGARET TOWNER

CRAP SHOOT

Consider my mother
who always exercised,
ate greens from her garden,
but suffered strokes,
congestive heart failure,
a hip fracture,
spinal meningitis,
blood clots,
atrial fibrillation,
pneumonia,
two car accidents,
slow decimation of her mind.
Yet still alive at 94,
it's the luck of the draw
as she wonders whether
she'll make it to 100.

Or Lilly's grandfather
who never was ill
a day of his life,
caught a cold at 89,
took some antibiotics,
died a week later.

What about my brother
who gave us no warning,
dropped to the floor
from a heart attack
in the best days of his life.
No divine design
happening here.

And the woman
who was in Auschwitz?
What are the chances,
after surviving the death camp,
that she could survive again
until she was 97 years old?

All I can do is nurture hope,
that I will beat the odds,
hope that I too can survive
a few more random
rolls of the dice.

MARGARET TOWNER

RISE AND FALL OF LIFE

The three-tiered plant hanger
is on the patio where my mother
could see it from her chair
when she was still living
in the house. Barb hung it high
last year and placed three
bright pots of graduated size:
one white flowering plant
at the top, in constant bloom,
a jade plant in the middle
always pale green, and finally
a red blooming succulent
with flowers that come and go.

DALE SPROWL

OUR FATHER'S FOUR SEASONS

Trips to the tracks,

our father's four seasons,

      Hollywood Park,

      Los Alamitos,

      Del Mar,

      Santa Anita.

Green odds boards and steno pads,

the System—

      the one that would beat the odds,

      cut our losses,

      achieve incremental gains—

our family's profit and loss statement.

BARBARA EKNOIAN

PRINCE AND PAUPER

My father couldn't have known
when he composed a poem
for Jackie Kennedy
about little John-John's last salute,
that his own three-year-old son,
would have something
in common with John-John.

They shared the same birthday
month and year, November 1960.
Both of them died during 1999
in their prime at thirty-nine,
but there the likeness ends.

Handsome John Kennedy, Jr., crashed
when he piloted his own private plane
near Martha's Vineyard.
Three months later,
my brother overdosed
in a rundown Long Beach motel
without any green in his pockets.

Fate is so often unkind.
Yet, pictures remain of both of them
when they were happy school boys.
Their world was an open opportunity.
My brother's hope to be a comedian;
John Kennedy, Jr., a noble gentleman.

SYED AFZAL HAIDER

HOW GREEN WAS MY VALLEY

Thus whispered the oozing drops of dew this morning in the grove
'The flowering garden remains full of blossom, whither goes the dew.'

Khwaja Mir Dard

After putting his infant son David to bed, Mitka sat in David's room thinking of the time when he used to read, every night, bedtime stories to his older son Matthew, and what a distressing time that was. Matthew had lost his mother, Iris, when he was two.

Matthew was now eleven, and Mitka was married again, father of two-year-old David. But, unlike with Matthew, Mitka rarely read bedtime stories to David. He only did it on a given night, if Holly, his wife, David's mother, was busy. Melanie the babysitter read David stories and put him to sleep every Friday night when Holly and Mitka went out. With Matthew, Mitka had no choice, so he did. With David he has a choice, so he doesn't.

Mitka stared out at the back entrance of a neighbor's house, a yellow bug-catcher light attached to the porch flickered, and the moth that flew into it got zapped instantly.

✈

In the creative writing class that Mitka taught, Brian Z. read a story that was well written, but with a bit too many details. The story had to do with fear of flying and crash of a DC-10. "A jumbo jet landing in light snow, on its way down, knocked the globe off of Globe Life Insurance. A big bang and boom, then thick dark clouds and flame and the acrid smell of fuel." Mitka's ears rang as he listened and tried to stay in focus to the voices around the table, but the faces blurred.

Many years ago, Iris had died in a plane crash.

Mikka was thirty-six and Iris was thirty-one. Matthew was two years and four days old. Mitka, a writer, a writer of pain of everyday living, continued to write. It was too late for him to be a silver screen hero.

May Lord have mercy upon us. Tomorrow we shall all die.

He wiped the sweat from his forehead with the palm of his hand, combed his hair back with his fingers on a cold day in late May, and called off the class early.

✈

On the home front, Holly left for Phoenix with David for five days to visit her sister Lily.

✈

After Iris's death, Mitka turned into total nothing, and day after day he killed her plants. He over-watered, under-watered, and fed too much Miracle-Gro to her begonias, Boston ferns, elephant's foot, the zebra plant, and her baby's breath. The green turned into dust.

Jai Ho, Praise Be, the only source of life in the face of Iris's death was her baby. Matthew, their son, needed his mother and he needed his father. There was pain—the past was too laborious to contemplate and the future was too hard to comprehend. But there was present to deal with every day, and the need to be a father, with concerns for childcare, meals, laundry, matching socks, doctors' appointments, all the details that filled the day. There was no time to ask why—only to do. Mitka assumed the task of being a father with the frenzy of a madman, flying off in every direction, two steps ahead, and three steps behind, four minutes early and five minutes late. Like a defeated boxer, he wanted to stay down, but he woke early and stayed up late. There was an absence of luminosity. Mitka didn't want to add more to the existing darkness, and left the lights on in the nighttime so Matthew wouldn't be sleeping in the dark.

Matthew started to read the bedtime stories on his own when he was in first grade. Resting against a large stuffed pillow with yellow, red, and blue toy cars printed on it, holding his book, *The Velveteen Rabbit* by Margery Williams, he read, "Somebody has to love you for a long, long time, for you to become real." Mitka said nothing. Missing Iris, he looked at his son for a long moment. He kissed Matthew's forehead and told him, "I love you." He tucked in his son and walked out, controlling a sob.

He looked at a photograph of Iris that he'd taken on a spring vacation in Paris before Matthew was born. She stood there in lush green la Cimetière du Père-Lachaise on a cool sunny day in front of Chopin's grave. She looked fabulous, appearing full of joy, her large brown eyes turned toward the camera, her lovely smile enchanting, her dark lustrous hair cut short make her look like she was eighteen. She read Malamud, Fowles, and Joyce Carol Oates, believed in reincarnation, and wanted to be cremated. She disappeared without saying goodbye, now only a photograph on the mantle. Emptiness has no boundaries.

Lost and uncertain, still, in love with what's not there, green was my valley once.

End the endlessness.

✈

In the morning, Mitka was wandering around in his slippers staring out the dirty window, when Ace Baba, a writer friend, called to ask how he was doing in the wake of the latest plane crash.

A United Airlines flight from Denver to Chicago crashed in Sioux City. One hundred and eighty-four people survived the crash, a miracle. But one hundred and twelve died.

CBS News, Channel 2 at six p.m., wanted Ace to offer a retrospective on the crash that killed five local writers, including Iris, on their way to a writer's conference in L.A. Ace wanted to know if it would be all right for him to talk about Iris.

"Every other week there is a new plane crash. I can never keep them straight," Mitka told Ace. "Go ahead, talk about it. After all, it's been many long years now."

"Can you meet for lunch today?" asked Ace.

"Yes."

Today was Iris's birthday. She would have turned forty.

✈

Listening to the car radio, during their short ride to school, Matthew learned of the latest plane crash.

"My mother died in a plane crash," he said.

Mitka nodded and turned off the radio. He'd never found the right way to talk to Matthew about the plane crash that had killed his mother. Once Matthew seemed too young, then too old. When he was little, over three years old, he asked Mitka who was his Mommy and where was she. Mitka didn't know what the age-appropriate answer was, so he blurted out the truth. "Your mother died in a plane crash." That made both of them fearful of flying.

"What do the captains of planes on the way to crashing announce to their passengers?" Matthew asked abruptly.

"I don't know," Mitka said, "but I would like to think that at a moment like that they would announce the truth. 'We are about to flip over and take a nosedive. Say your prayers, please.'"

Mitka made a right on Dodge Avenue. They rode in silence for the next few blocks listening to the sound of the road under the tires. He dropped Matthew off at the school and watched him walk along with the other boys and girls, his lunch pail swinging. He wondered if he should have let Matthew know that today was his mother's birthday. How much should Matthew know? Which details, Mitka wondered. Or should he mourn Iris, Matthew's mother, alone? When Mitka thinks of motherhood, he wants to cry—not for his sake. He had a mother and a good one, too. What makes him cry is the thought that he has a son who is growing up without his mother. Why does Mathew have no mother?

✈

Singsong chants of his prayer. *Jai Ho*, Praise Be, the source of life prevailed in the face of Iris's death. Matthew and Mitka survived. Concerns for future and regrets of past, that's how we think and plan our lives. We rarely live or dream in present or understand the timeless considerations of human conditions, and we rarely see the whole picture. Accidents happen.

In life...and life, Mitka's dark hair, from occasional silver back then had turned to salt and pepper, and his waist from thirty-five to an even thirty-two. Mitka got older and thinner, but he didn't die from the death of Iris. He let it be. "Somebody has to love you for a long, long time for you to become real."

A single yellow tulip blossomed in Iris's garden, but once there had been so many flowers, of many colors and many hues.

✈

The sun and rain played hide and seek, bright and sunny one moment, dark and cloudy the next. For so late in May, the merry month of May, it was cold, filled with life, chock full of blossoms, flourishing green, fully dressed, but empty and naked inside.

Mitka rushed to meet Ace for lunch.

It had been many years down the road, and Mitka now felt awkward bringing up Iris's death or her death anniversary to anybody.

During their lunch, Ace Baba asked Mitka, "How does it feel, not to have secrets any more?" Mitka looked at Ace, tanned and handsome, built like a Marine, face lined and leathered, blond hair flecked with gray. After all these years, Ace still remembered Iris and always talked about her.

"I am the Buffalo Soldier," Mitka said, "fighting for I don't know what."

"One lives with the past, not necessarily in it."

Mitka took a gulp of his ouzo and said, "I do live a pretty good life. I am married again and I have another child. I love them. And I have not lost my lust for life or my sense of desire and pleasure. There is not an absence of joy. My sadness is my state of life. It may be sad and gloomy. My grief is not a major depression or desolation any more. It's just a continuous melancholy."

"O, a thoughtful and gentle sadness," Ace mimicked. "You haven't let Iris die, you haven't forgiven Iris for dying on you. And you have not forgiven yourself. Your love of today finds no place to nest in the deserted ruins of yesterday's love. You live life with the guilt of a survivor."

"No, I do not feel guilty. Numb. Frozen. Deadened. Isolated. Damaged." Mitka looked Ace in the eyes and said, "I have loved before, and I'm trying to love again. I'm doing the best I can with what I got dealt, and I think I play a good game. Satisfy my soul, nothing can for now. Sometimes I feel an urge to let blood flow from my veins. Not to kill myself, just to feel the pain or lack of it. Emptiness is a disease, a cancer of the soul that ultimately kills you. Love is easy."

"In the soul of a dry seed waits the miracle of life, green, an evergreen tomorrow," said Ace.

It's easy to slip. It's effortless to fall.

Holly and David returned from their trip. David scampered towards Mitka, his tiny feet moving haphazardly, unevenly, and calling, "Daddy, Daddy." Mitka picked him up and held him in his arms. Matthew and Holly joined them in a huddle for a group hug. Mitka was happy for the moment.

CLIFTON SNIDER

A LAST GOODBY

For Evan Allan Snider
3 January 1992

No cremated remains of you, my elder
brother, on this, your fiftieth birthday.
No minute traces of skin, no bones, no teeth.
Still clueless, we order your name
engraved in granite. Nearby your father lies
mingled in dirt, the same name
exposed to the same sun, wind, rain.

Green hills, green ocean, green bridge
across the L.A. harbor—these your engraved letters
will watch, like a spirit, every day. Perhaps
a thousand years from now somewhere
some strange people will uncover
your nameless skeleton. What clue
will tell them someone murdered you
at thirty-four? What clue but your name
can say to whom or what you belonged,
in what century you disappeared,
who loved you?

Granite lives longer than flesh,
so to granite we commit your name
and say a last good-bye, beloved son & brother.
Rest well, wherever you are.

—from *Moonman: New and Selected Poems*
(World Parade Books, 2012)

TERE SIEVERS

THE SWEATER
Late fall,
to stave off the chill,
I pull down the green sweater
I gave to my father,
the one thing of him
I kept after he died.
This year
I notice an unraveling at the sleeves
and tiny pinholes
right at the heart.

KENDALL STEINLE

SHEEPSKIN

The sun was tired,
resting just above the houses which made South Bend
look like it was going up in flames.
It was the last night before everyone grew up, my brother
first, but I too. Attempting to go out with a bang,
we carried in the stuff that I couldn't touch,
yearning for one more night of freedom before
the sheepskin was placed in his hands, signifying
the end of an era that cannot be explained nor understood.
I stood face to face with Jesus earlier that evening,
separated by tape marked with a word telling me stand back;
He was broken and cracked and everyone needs some space
        every now and then.
(There was another Jesus in that town too, arms open wide.
We are champions.)
There's nothing like summer, like an end,
like being that much closer to going home.
We walked, we danced, we had the weather to seal the night.
We held hands, breathing it all in.
We informed the elderly neighbor behind us of our evening plans,
pleading with our eyes to let us be loud, awful kids for just one
more night. Just one more night, please.
Something loomed behind her eyes, something undetectable.
She watched the town burn behind us, only
brought back to reality when attacked by my brother's
thrift store Army coat, that green that was so very, very red.
It was that deep dull olive, torn and tattered and purchased for
        under a dollar
with some stranger's name on the breast pocket.
Her wet eyes travelled from the bottom button to top,
        to my brother's face,
to each of our faces.
Stay out of the war, she said, quietly, gently, with a smile,
before closing the door in front of our crooked eyebrows.
I left the fun later that night to go back and sit with Jesus.
It was all about to change, it was all about to end.

➤

I stood up, stepped over the yellow tape, and whispered into His ear
what the angel had told me; the pertinent information that could
save the rest of the world from the same fate. The words of a savior.
Back at the house, back in the midst of bodies swinging
back and forth and side to side,
back to the liquids that make people forget that anything is wrong, ever,
back to guitars and football and big, big plans, I returned.
When sunlight crawled over our backs and faces and told us
    it was time to go,
we left, my brother first, but I too,
and not empty-handed.
I held between my arms a shield,
a shield to endure the years that I had left to face.
I made it a promise to the man that I would tell everyone. Everyone.
I wrote it on paper bills, personal checks, peoples' mailboxes,
and a window of my high school, its message now a puzzle
in the rubble of my Alma mater. I shouted it from the top of
    the tallest tree
and I danced it out on every grave in Akron—even the ones not yet
filled.
I'll say it to strangers, I'll whisper it into my daughter's ear,
I'll inhale it, I'll exhale it.
I'll cry it and shout it and laugh it and bleed it.
I'll hum it in my sleep.
I'll stay out of the war.

TIM WELLS

THE HORROR OF YOUR DAUGHTER'S NEW BOYFRIEND TURNING UP WEARING GREEN SUEDE CUBAN HEELS

If that's not enough he's also in an open necked white shirt.
Wide enough that you see his nipples. It fair cuts a dash.
All in all, it's way too Errol Flynn. Much as I like him
I don't want Errol Flynn around nineteen year old girls.

My troublesome daughter's friend, looks me in the eye then rolls hers
Clockwise from quarter to, to half past and ends peering into his shirt
before leaning close and whispering, 'His nipples are saying *'Love me.''*
I differ and suggest they're rather saying *"I would go out tonight
but I haven't got a stitch to wear."*

The conversation is awkward, my face has said it all,
but I can see an effort being made and if he's doing that
to please the girl he can't be so bad. Her friends chip in
with jokes and stories to help us meet on middle ground.

Beer makes company amiable, and concord established
I'm thinking he'll reconsider the shoes in future. Mid joke, he mistakenly
lifts and drains my pint. My face moves from 1950s disapproving dad
to medieval. Later that week a shirt is torn in the laundry, toast
falls on suede, butter side down.

CLINT MARGRAVE

FAMILY TREE

It was in Missouri,
during the late nineteenth century.

There were three brothers—
my great, great uncles.

One served in the House,
one in the Senate,

the other got hanged for
stealing a horse.

Previously published in 3AM (UK)

LORI MCGINN

WOMAN WITH A GREEN OLIVE, FLOATING

Mom,

Do you remember?

There was that time

You were all fashion savvy,

With your martini,

your fancy cigarette holder?

Pall Mall cigarette poised.

There was a pool, a party,

Me, at the bottom of the pool

looking up, wondering when to breathe.

JOAN JOBE SMITH

GREEN WHEN IT RAINED

When it rained was when my mother sang
her sweetest as she cooked supper in the
kitchen. "Ohh," she'd whisper, fogging up
the window with her breath. "Look at the
beautiful rain, how green the world, the
leaves, when it rains. Rain now means
food to eat next year. Do you understand?"
No, I didn't. We lived in Southern California
in the 1950s in the eternal plentitude midst of
supermarkets, farmers markets selling food
grown in nearby cornfields and orange groves.
Dairies with fat cows surrounded us, jingling
ice cream men and bakery trucks filled with
sweets and hot bread drove up and down
our streets. In between her songs, Amapola,
my pretty little poppy, you'll never know
how much I love you, always, she'd tell me
of yellow Texas droughts and brown famine
how she searched shadow gullies for greens
when she was a little girl, stole corn, peaches
and pecans from rich folks' fields and orchards.
I'd never gone hungry nor had to steal or search
for my food and her sweet soprano tales of
hunger filled me with so much wanting that come
suppertime as I mashed the buttery, Texas-style
potatoes, I scraped spotless the pot with the spoon
to lick every speck, grateful to all the gods
of cornucopia, ambrosia, and green Mother Rain.

PAUL KAREEM TAYYAR

THE JESUIT

You were the sound of the boardwalk on the night before the Fourth of July.

You were the sound of the sinner's voice on the morning after confession.

You were the sound of the troubadour's guitar at the bridge of a song

      Where the soldier survived.

You were the sound of the lover's monologue when the stage had been emptied

      Of love.

You were the sound of the mother's prayers as she placed a flower on the tomb

      Of her child.

You were the sound of the husband who turned in his sleep towards a wife

      Who was no longer there.

You were the sound of the running of bison across a green prairie.

You were the sound of the burning page in a book whose poems had been committed

      To memory.

You were the sound of the river where old men fished for their long-vanished youths.

MARC MALANDRA

EX-PAT RETURNS HOME TO FAMILY ABSENCES AND CALIFORNIA, WHICH CAN'T SHAKE PARADISE EVEN IN MID-WINTER

1.

The stone path to the garden,
nasturtiums rising like tiny suns
up the hedges, ice plant fingers
pointing up from the bluffs:
It's hard to imagine grief
in a more beautiful location.

Several years ago, just across
the hill, trailer homes slid
down into the canyon,
left a scar on the hillside,
a sign with a warning.

2.

Grandparents traced the family
tree's roots, discovering
our Italian family seal.
Though current relatives
live in the mountains of Abruzzo,
there was a seahorse on the crest
pointing to a seafaring past
or at least dreams of wandering
the waterways of the earth.

3.

When Grandpa died, Dad bought a boat,
Grandma got a cat, named it
"Tangee" for its orange fur,
but I thought *tangential*, which
is how she seemed to feel,
alone in the too-large house.
Rabbits and hummingbirds
scatter outside the windows.
His paintings haunt the walls.

➤

4.

My dad is learning to pilot his boat.
He still talks about the "speedometer,"
"parking" in the slip.
The sea seems large enough
to lose his loss in. He wants
to teach me how to sail.

5.

I imagine snow in Tokyo
while I sit on Grandma's front porch,
sunshine on my face, bird songs
blanketing the air as dew
has the lawns. Before me
eucalyptus limbs twist
into the air, a dance
in motion so slow it eludes us.

I don't want to see them
in terms of bodies, yet I can't
help feeling these trees are
our taller more graceful selves,
more loyal to soil than sky,
rooted, but reaching higher.

PART XIII

TREES

ERLE KELLY

MAGNOLIA RULES

Arms of a Botero woman,
her thick limbs stretch out,
giving shade, coolness;
nemesis to flower or plant
that cannot outlast
the shadow she casts.

Fern, calla lily, impatiens,
staghorn, clivia, primrose thrive.
Periwinkle, cosmos, marigold,
poppy struggle for light.

Her scented petals
tower above her domain,
difficult to see, out of reach.
She sheds spiny brown cones
as her only gift.

When laced,
this eighty-year old
madam of the yard
rests the eye,
cuts intricate patterns
with clouds against
red twilight sky.

JANE BUEL BRADLEY

EVERGREEN PEAR

The old tree started to grow up
then turned left and grew a while
before it decided to go right—but always
upward, you understand,
spreading its branches out
to embrace the air,
climbing far above the roof.

Early spring gives it a special glory,
weaving a veil of frail white petals
over the whole tree.
A gusty wind then can turn
the blossoms into a blizzard,
the only kind that ever visits
my California garden.

The rough black trunk is so thick
it might push the house over some day.
The leaves, oval to a point
and pinked along the edges,
assume a coral red in autumn,
and when they fall,
cover the ground with a bright fire.
I feel I could sleep warm under them
for a night,
               or forever.

JANE BUEL BRADLEY

EUCALYPTUS

The big eucalyptus in my alley
has a wrinkled trunk;
bark hangs in fraying ropes from
smooth branches, apricot color
brushed with green.

Today I pick up three crescents
from the swirl of leaves on the ground.
They feel like parchment in my hand,
and the seedbox under my foot
sends up a sharp fragrance.

I smelled it first as a child, coming
from Missouri to California,
choked up with asthma.
That fragrance, mixed with sea air,
cleared the way right down
to the bottom of my lungs
so I could take a deep breath
at last and sing.

DONNA HILBERT

TREES

Larry, if you hear the crowds cheer
know it's for the boys,
basketball champs this year.
Larry's Wizards, in your memory,
emblazoned on their backs.
They're growing like trees:
the palm tree on the peninsula
planted for you,
and the Nature Center's sycamore
so hardy it will grow to a canopy
like the sycamore shading our first house,
La Carta Circle, Dear Heart, remember?
Remember the house, the street, the tree,
our three babies,
lives branching out before us
a limitless haven of green.

AL BASILE

AFTER THE GROUP, THE INDIVIDUAL

Nature's gold at first is green,
last solid color to be seen.
The single-minded leaves agree
to stand together on the tree—
until a voice of ice is heard
to whisper a divisive word.
The dawn arrives when each leaf finds
the chill's instilled a change of mind;
then scarlet-tinted, many-hued,
each burns according to its mood,
and proving rules about perfection
(a private choice available to all
which when attained must bring about a fall)
insists on making its exception.

DANIEL MCGINN

LEAFY MOMENTS (A BAKERS DOZEN)

I
I bought a tree online.
It arrived the next morning
fully equipped with leaves.

II
One week later
I received an e-mail
from one of the leaves
asking for more water.

III
This leaf
became a spokesleaf
for the others.

IV
The sun shines
through the window.

The leaf is green.
Light is warmth.
Alive is good.

V
The leaf is on the tree.
The tree is on the table.
Kermit is on the TV
strumming on the old banjo.

VI
My parakeet
cocks its head
and ponders the leaf.
The leaf
is shaped
like a feather.

➤

VII
Take the tree outside.
Here comes the wind.
The leaf gets all excited
and starts wagging its tail.

VIII
Soil and roots are one.
Tree and leaf are one.
Sun and milk are one.
Breakfast for everybody!

IX
Evening shadows fall on the leaf.

X
A blackbird sleeps
on the windowsill;
in the blink of an eye
it opens its wings.

XI
The green leaf stands up
like an arrowhead.
All of its fountains
have turned into gold.

XII
Frost and window are one.
Stem and branch were one.
Leaf and air are one.

XIII
The leaf has leapt.
The room is full of circles.

Gerard Manley Hopkins

BINSEY POPLARS

My aspens dear, whose airy cages quelled,

Quelled or quenched in leaves the leaping sun,

All felled, felled, are all felled;

Of a fresh and following folded rank

Not spared, not one

That swam or sank

On meadow and river and wind-wandering

weed-winding bank.

O if we but knew what we do

When we delve or hew—

Hack and rack the growing green!

 Since country is so tender

To touch, her being so slender,

That, like this sleek and seeing ball

But a prick will made no eye at all,

Where we, even where we mean

To mend her we end her,

When we hew or delve:

After-comers cannot guess the beauty been.

Ten or twelve, only ten or twelve

Strokes of havoc unselve

The sweet especial scene,

Rural scene, a rural scene,

Sweet especial rural scene.

BENJAMIN MYERS

LOGGING IN SCOUT ROCK WOODS

The simple repetition of
the blade
jawing through
the trunk;

the gently falling flecks
of sawdust -
the heft and roll
of lumber.

BENJAMIN MYERS

A TIMBER TEMPLE

Once there were so many trees
you could cross England without so much as
touching the earth.

So many damn trees.

They held hands from the North Sea to the Irish Sea
from John O'Groats to
the other place;
trees,
a
sea
of them.

Rustling
rippling
swaying
whispering

in
a green cathedral
a timber temple
an infinite arboretum.

STEVEN KUHN

WEST

In the afternoon, she came to me.

Red wine summer spirit.
Strawberries and citronella.

In the 4:00 lull, the trees rested their thousand tongues,
deciding instead to think for a while
on whatever it is trees have to think about,

and we talked then,
of sacred things like shadows
and symmetry,
of caffeine and buzzing insects and quiet.

I think a tree's only thoughts are ancient praises.
When they sing, the song is a patient one,
and when they are tired,
they dream of summers past.
Trees are largely unconcerned.
Trees are never bored.

"The cool of the evening."
I've always loved that phrase.

When the sacred shadows began their tired push for dominance,
she brushed my cheek and departed
to the prolonged thunder of a plane headed west.
She again became the wind, and I again myself,
and tired. With all the old ghosts for company.

The trees stirred, dreaming, fitful,
About whatever it is that trees have to dream about,
and the contrail of a 747 became a streaking comet in the light of a sun
that seemed to be larger when it touched the horizon.

LeeAnne McIlroy Langton

THE TREE OF KNOWLEDGE

I noticed that most of my students
Were gazing longingly out the window
On an unusually beautiful
Southern California morning
I paused in my lecture to discover
That they were collectively noticing the unusual fruit
Exploding on the tree just outside our window
"What kind of fruit is *that?*"
They wondered with more curiosity than
They had ever shown for Plato or Rousseau
And so I told them about the pomegranate
How according to the Q'uran, it filled the gardens of paradise
How its image had once adorned the temples of Solomon
How it doomed Persephone to Hades
How it symbolizes prosperity and fertility in Hinduism
How it came here to us:
From the Iranian Plateaus to Turkey
Across the Mediterranean and transported across the oceans
By the Spanish conquistadors
How the city of Kandahar—now bombed and ravaged—
Was once reputed to have the finest pomegranates in the world
I told them that this was my favorite tree
And then we all went outside for a moment—
To marvel at this tree
Just staring for a moment
While the wind blew
Across our faces, a tender caress across the ages
And then the moment was gone—
The next day I walked into class
And someone, anonymously, had placed a single pomegranate
On my desk at the front of the class,
An altar before thirty students,
All newly baptized—
The red stain of pomegranate seeds outlining
Their smiles

PART XIV

NEW LIFE

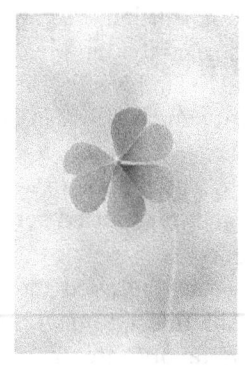

WILLIAM BLAKE

THE ECHOING GREEN

The sun does arise,
And make happy the skies.
The merry bells ring
To welcome the spring.
The skylark and thrush,
The birds of the bush,
Sing louder around,
To the bells' cheerful sound,
While our sports shall be seen
On the echoing green.

Old John with white hair
Does laugh away care,
Sitting under the oak,
Among the old folk.
They laugh at our play,
And soon they all say:
"Such, such were the joys
When we all, girls and boys,
In our youth-time were seen
On the echoing green."

Till the little ones weary
No more can be merry;
The sun does descend,
And our sports have an end.
Round the laps of their mother
Many sisters and brothers,
Like birds in their nest,
Are ready for rest;
And sport no more seen
On the darkening green

JONNE RHODES

TRANSPARENCIES

When you were rolling back
and forth in my belly re-shaping
my little ribcage into the apple
barrel it is today,
and enlarging the altered heart
I carry now for life,
I used to go out to our fenced
rectangle of yellowed grass,
lay a thin towel
out under the white sky
behind our apartment,
and undress.

Lying flat, I speak to you as I float
scarf after scarf across
the impossible globe
that contains you.

"This is your Momma who loves you,"
I sing, pulling the chiffons.
I whisper,
"Green, baby, green.
Here's blue, baby, blue."
And then, with the music,
"Red, red, red do you hear it?"

JESSICA BROWN

THOUGHTS ON A COMING BABY

If there is a break in the astonishment
—in the stunned, frozen fear—
there unfurls something else,

the way in cracks of old cement sidewalks
springs small dainty clover
or the rip in a brown hillside
brings ferns, mossy and fan-like, a dell.

So unfurls this, deep and green—

somehow, I can trust this body.

When there is a baby in the house
waiting to be nuzzled,

there too will be, astonishingly,
—leaves and buds aplenty—
a mother there,
rising from folds of unfurling self
to meet him.

JOHN BRANTINGHAM

THE GREEN OF SUNSET

I saw your sonogram this morning, heard your heartbeat for the first time, and it got me thinking about life, how long it is, how much happens to one person. I wished you health and happiness, of course, but thinking about you fifty years from now, I mostly hoped the world would not make you disappointed and bitter. If life does beat you down, I hope you realize bitterness comes only from moments that stick out in our minds like pustules on a tongue. We chew on them, give them an importance they don't have to have, forget that anything else exists. I hope you remember that there are good times too, beautiful times, and more importantly there are all those moments in between the good and the bad. That's what life is, those moments in between—like when a sunset goes from orange to green. People forget the green of sunset because it's not as dramatic as the orange burst at the end of the day or the void of black at the beginning of the evening, but it's there for a second we all ignore. If you find you have become bitter on your fiftieth birthday, I want you to dwell not so much on the great loves and graduations as on the trip to the supermarket when you had a craving for a kiwi fruit or the long walk home from school when you just thought about your day. I hope you remember that there are so many green moments you will have forgotten, as you will most certainly forget what happened today, for these moments inside your mother, these moments you will not be able to remember, are just as important and just as real as any other moment. Today, you danced inside your mother because she drank orange juice. If you ever become bitter, remember that there was a moment today when we all watched you dance your orange juice dance and listened to your orange juice heart and though you cannot remember it, you heard your father's voice through the thin flap of your mother's stomach as he said, "My beautiful child, I love you, I love you, I love you."

PAUL KAREEM TAYYAR

LITTLE MYTHOLOGIES

This is the hour of the sundial,

The green lake and the lady who defends it,

This is the hour of the rose and the watercolor clouds,

This is the hour when the angels,

Long crippled by an absence of faith in those they have been sent to protect,

Awake to find that the children are holding their arms out to them,

And the white rain warms its hands by the slow fire of an emerging sun.

Here is where your life becomes a silent film,

Where your life becomes a long poem filled with lovely metaphors,

Where you no longer have to dream about what the days before you will become,

This is the hour that you had been promised,

See your dreams sitting like starlings upon the telephone wires

Across the street from where you stand.

NOTES FROM THE AUTHORS

JENA ARDELL ("Spring Sings"): I took a Polaroid I shot, a vintage illustration by Gyo Fujikawa, and a poem by Sara Teasdale and remixed them. The original poem was titled "April." (The roofs are shining from the rain. /The sparrows twitter as they fly, /And with a windy April grace/ The little clouds go by.//Yet the backyards are bare and brown With only one unchanging tree—/I could not be so sure of Spring/Save that it sings in me.) I cut the Teasdale poem into pieces, rearranged the words, omitted others, and completely changed the meaning.

AL BASILE: This poem (**"Maya's First Hard Boiled Egg"**) is a recent versification of a scene from my unpublished second novel *Memories of You,* written forty years ago. I work in smaller forms most of the time nowadays, but I always liked that little episode from the book and decided to recast it. The first line of **"After the Group, the Individual"** is an inversion of Frost. As a native New Englander, I grew up with Frost as a local hero of sorts. Like him, I write mostly in blank verse and attempt to disguise my labor under a conversational tone. I do believe that the underlying metric spine heightens the language, but you might be unaware of it if you heard me read.

PATRICK DELANEY ("Spring Rain"): Uncle Larry's swamp is just that. It is his escape from a cold, maniacal wife, his conscience, and more than anything his children, who haunt him like ghosts. As an orphan, I am allowed into this world and he sees me as a part of it, like the dragonfly. This painting is outlined in water. He drains the water, as if purging himself, but it fills up again and again. I am drawn to the water he is compelled to remove. This story is part of an unfinished novel.

MERRILL FARNSWORTH: Much of my writing begins in The Writing Circle, a series of workshops I've designed to inspire writers of all levels to connect with authentic voice. We circle up weekly on the fourth floor of a converted convent in Nashville, Tennessee. The unique shape each poem, essay or work of fiction can take from one common prompt always amazes me. When writers create from a cauldron of experience exquisitely and excruciatingly their own, somehow a universal chord is struck and we all go out into the world uplifted.

SYED AFZAL HAIDER ("How Green Was My Valley"): First of all, I must say that I find it a challenge to write on a theme, the need to touch on the given subject in some way. In early days of my learning to write, to write on a given theme was a like answering a test question and it still is. For me to write and justify a given theme is to somehow define or redefine the given question in some way that I could answer and then find a unique narrative to answer it. My writing comes from some sad and depressed place, from lost domain, something gone. For example, green is all you say [in the anthology guidelines]—money, the environment, Irish luck, youthful inexperience, the hope of spring—they are all valid explorations. To me, green also represents birth—birth of the new and rebirth of what is gone and lost, both the opening of new wounds and sprouting of new life in spring after the killing winter. But we cannot address birth and rebirth without dealing with loss and the ultimate loss—death. And this is where I found my story.

ZACK HUNTER ("Hypogymnia Physodes"): Sent from an Android device.

MICHAEL C. KEITH ("Steaks of Wrath"): This story originally appeared in *The Greensilk Journal* and was nominated for a Pushcart Prize.

MORIAH LACHAPELL ("Green" and "Dictation"): I spent my teenage years in a Messianic cult. I am still recovering. Much of my writing is a reflection on gender, sexuality, loss, religion, and self-identity.

LEEANNE MCILROY LANGTON: Any poem I have ever written is because of Paul Kareem Tayyar. Mostly I write essays and journals, and when Tayyar suggested poetry to me I scoffed and made some smart-ass comment. That anyone other than myself takes any interest whatsoever in my writing still baffles me. I write to (try to) process and organize my own interior worlds—specifically my emotions—which are decidedly disorganized and at times overwhelming. I write for myself. I am usually writing when I am, as my daughters and I say, "feeling my feelings." The structural organization that is demanded from essays helps me to organize and process my feelings a little. This was most obvious in a piece I wrote for my local newspaper covering the funeral of a young boy whom I knew—the agony of watching his family say goodbye to him was unbearable. The public response to that article encouraged me to publish more, that despite the self-centeredness of writing, it can have a public value as well. The fluidity and freedom from strict organization that poetry offers allows me to feel less tame with my emotions. Poetry captures a moment that may defy organization or process. It just "is." Writing a poem lets me express something without necessarily having to explain or understand it.

ELLARAINE LOCKIE ("Autopsy Means to See with One's Own Eyes"): When the editor asked to know more about the poem, this was my answer: "Yes, I can see why you would have mixed feelings about this poem. I had a greenish, queasy feeling while writing it, which is why it came to mind for a green theme. What inspired the poem was that I started thinking one day about what exactly is involved with an autopsy. I began my research with the definition of the word and was taken aback by it: "to see with one own's eyes." With those words, I was off and running with the poem, which won the Writecorner Press Poetry Prize the year I wrote it.

KAREN MARGOLIS ("I Am a Hill of Poetry"): This poem is part of a cycle in progress. The title of this cycle is taken from *The Song of Amergin*: "...said to have been chanted by the chief bard of the Milesian invaders as he set foot on the soil of Ireland in the year of the world 2376 (1268 B.C.E)." Written originally in Old Goidelic, the only surviving versions are in colloquial Irish translation. The phrase "I am a hill of poetry" represents knowledge and is assigned to the month of September, which has the vine as its tree and is the month of the titmouse and the poet, "the least abashed of men as the titmouse is the least easily abashed of birds. Both band together in companies in this month and go on circuit in search of a liberal hand; and as the titmouse climbs spirally up a tree, so the poet also spirals to immortality. And Variegated is the colour of the titmouse, and of the Master-poet's dress." (Quotes from *The White Goddess* by Robert Graves.) This cycle of thirteen poems is based on the lunar calendar Robert Graves describes in *The White Goddess*. Each month is associated with specific natural/mystical characteristics and a particular tree. The cycle consists of a poem for each month based on a particular person's birth date and character. So far, I have written five of the thirteen poems.

DANIEL MCGINN: The poem "**Outside**" was first published by The Inevitable Press, in *Wall*: Chapbook #102, part of the Laguna Poets series. "**Leafy Moments (A Baker's Dozen)**" was written after reading the Wallace Stevens poem "**Thirteen Ways of Looking at a Blackbird**"; it was recently published by *Write Bloody* in my book of poems, *1000 Black Umbrellas*. The poem "**Mornings at our House**" is published for the first time in the **Silver Birch Press** *Green Anthology*.

TERE SIEVERS ("Monarch"): Some times it's a long wait at the bus stop for the Muse to arrive. The prompt from the editor for the *Green Anthology* was a welcome arrival. Many hours have been spent with my grandchildren in the front yard, watching the Monarch's transformation. As my six-year-old granddaughter exclaimed, "I love those butterflies so much"—and so do I.

JOAN JOBE SMITH ("Chicago"): This poem was originally published in my chapbook, *A Spy in a Broccoli Forest*, which was the Sheila-Na-Gig 1st Place Competition Winner, 1996.

PHILIP VERMAAS ("The Passing Stranger"): When I'm trying to capture the nature of a weighty scene from my own life, one that usually has to do with the "cruelty of loveless love," and I'm not yet far enough from it, I sometimes write fables. That way I don't have to worry about accurately representing character but let the fantastical elements serve as suggestions for typical human qualities. It's an expedient way to deal with the marrow and discard the unwieldy jumble of as yet unsettled details. I wrote "The Passing Stranger" during the nasty end of a relationship. I was busy entertaining the feeling that the possibility of love returned was an illusion, that I was learning this lesson and so wouldn't be as shortsighted next time. But the Pink Man learns a lesson that makes him grey. It is not the lesson he might have learned, simply a reaction that leads to a safe blindness which he would have done better to avoid—for his own sake and the sake of the flower. The Grey Man has missed the point and the possibility of love dies.

MELANIE VILLINES ("Green Fluorescent Glow"): This story follows "Silver Bells, Silver Bells," included in the **Silver Birch Press** *Silver Anthology*. Both stories (part of an incomplete novel) are based on incidents that occurred during one of my first freelance jobs after moving to Los Angeles. Since I was the only woman in the mix (the clients and all the residents of the halfway house were men), I decided to make the main character a man—because I didn't want the story to come off as a "this is only happening to me because I'm a woman." A more accurate assessment would have been, "this is only happening to me because I'm a writer." Of course, I filtered the experience through the green river [see introduction] of my imagination—and it turned into something quite different. I gave the main character (Vance Middlebrooks) my reversed initials to maintain a connection to his dilemma. I have always admired the way Dickens christened his characters with memorable names and wanted to do something similar in this tale. I chose "Middlebrooks" as a nod to Dante's *Inferno* ("In the middle of the journey of our life I found myself in a dark wood..."). Griffin is the flying monster that represents all that is fake about L.A., and his last name "Gnowles" was a jokey way of saying "know less." And Dr. Bing...well, I just thought the name sounded funny.

FRED VOSS ("Sir Gawain Takes Out the Trash"): The poem appeared in *Ambit* (U.K.) 2011.

EDDIE WOODS: The title **("Green My Envy")** says it all, after which the text elaborates in excruciating detail. The poetess Marie Ponsot, to whom the poem is dedicated, became a close friend when I was in my later teens, in Jamaica, New York (as did her then-husband and father of their seven children, the French painter Claude Ponsot). She was also a mentor of sorts...for a while. Her first published book, *True Minds* (City Lights Pocket Poets Series, 1957), is exquisite. This was followed, many years later, by *Admit Impediment*. As for her mind... "I'm out of things to read," she said to me one afternoon. "May I come over and borrow some books from you?" She took five thick volumes, prose and poetry. And returned them the next day. "Which did you read?" I asked. "Why all of them, of course," came her casual reply. Wouldn't your envy be green? Marie holds a master's degree in seventeenth-century literature and has translated sixty-nine children's books from the French, as well as *The Fables of La Fontaine*. A liberal Catholic, she is equally fluent in Latin. Marie Ponsot, a truly remarkable lady. **"Clear Queer Green"** was penned in a moment of divine madness in Madras, India (1976). The late "crazy-wisdom" poet Roberto Valenza always insisted it was one of his favorite poems. If any reader can tell the author what it's all about, he'll be eternally grateful!

ABOUT THE AUTHORS

BARBARA ALFARO is a graduate of Goddard College and the American Academy of Dramatic Arts. She is the recipient of a Maryland State Arts Council Individual Artist Award for her play *Dos Madres*. Her poems and essays have appeared in various literary journals. The paperback edition of her poems called *Singing Magic* and the Kindle edition of her poetry titled *First Kiss* are available on Amazon. *Mirror Talk,* her memoir about a Catholic girlhood and working in theatre won the 2012 IndieReader Discovery Award for Best Memoir and is also available on Amazon. Visit Barbara's website at www.BarbaraAlfaro.net

JENA ARDELL is a freelance photographer and writer. Her photography has been exhibited worldwide and has appeared in numerous publications, including *Rolling Stone*, and can be found as the cover art to a handful of novels. She is a regular contributing writer and concert photographer for *L.A. Weekly*'s music and arts sections. Jena earned second place in the online feature category at the L.A. Press Club's National Entertainment Journalism Awards 2011 for her contribution to *L.A. Weekly*'s Coachella coverage. Jena is currently pursuing editorial photography and seeking a publisher for a children's book she penned during a cross-country train trip.

AL BASILE is a poet, singer/songwriter, and cornetist. He grew up in a park in Haverhill, Massachusetts, graduated from Phillips Academy in 1966, and in 1970 was first to receive a Master's degree from the Brown University Writing Program. He began his musical career as a cornet player with *Roomful of Blues* in 1973, and has worked with the Duke Robillard Band as a songwriter and recording member since 1990, appearing on twelve CDs and a DVD. His songs have been used in films and television and covered by such artists as Ruth Brown. He has released nine solo blues and roots CDs under his own name, the last five reaching the top fifteen on the Living Blues airplay charts in their year of release. Guest artists have included the Blind Boys of Alabama and jazz great Scott Hamilton. Basile has been nominated three times, in 2010, 2012, and 2013, for a Blues Music Award as best horn player. He taught full time at the Providence Country Day School in East Providence, Rhode Island, from 1980-2005 and since then has concentrated on his writing, performing, and recording.

L. FRANK BAUM (1856-1919) created one of the most popular books in American children's literature, *The Wonderful Wizard of Oz*, for which he wrote thirteen sequels. A prolific author, Baum wrote fifty-five novels, eighty-two short stories, and over two hundred poems, as well as movie scripts and essays.

WILLIAM BLAKE (1757-1827) was an English poet, painter, and printmaker. For the most part unrecognized during his lifetime, Blake is now considered one of the greatest poets of all time in any language. As a visual artist, he has been lauded by one art critic as "far and away the greatest artist Britain has ever produced."

JANE BUEL BRADLEY's first book, *World Alive,* appeared from PEARL Editions when she was eighty-nine years old, and was followed two years later by *Tree of Life.* Jane continued to write poetry until shortly before her death two months shy of her ninety-fourth birthday. Jane was a beloved children's librarian in Long Beach, California, a political and environmental activist, and an inspiration to all who knew her. She was the niece of Ernest Thayer, author of the beloved classic baseball poem "Casey at the Bat."

JOHN BRANTINGHAM's poetry and fiction have been published in hundreds of magazines and venues, including Garrison Keillor's *Writer's Almanac, PEARL, Tears in the Fence, Confrontation*, and *The Journal*. His books include *East of Los Angeles* and *Let Us All Pray to Our Own Strange Gods* (forthcoming from World Parade Books). He works at Mt. San Antonio College, where he teaches English and directs the creative writing programs.

JESSICA BROWN has an MFA in Fiction from Seattle Pacific University and an MA in English from Boston College. Sometimes composition professor, she is now working on her eighth novel. Her essay on Gerard Manley Hopkins was recently published in the *Journal for Spiritual Formation and Soul Care*, and her essay on Jane Austen's *Persuasion* is forthcoming in a book on Austen and the arts.

RACHEL CAREY is a writer and filmmaker. She received an MFA in Film Directing from NYU, an M.Ed. from Harvard, and a BA in English from Yale. She currently lives with her family in New Jersey and teaches college film classes. Silver Birch Press publish her debut novel, *Debt*, in February 2013.

CHRIS DAVIDSON's writing has appeared in *Zyzzyva, Alaska Quarterly Review, Burnside Review, Zocalo Public Square, The Rumpus, Jacket2*, and elsewhere. He teaches at Biola University and lives in Seal Beach, California, with his wife and sons.

PATRICK DELANEY lives in a suburb of Philadelphia with his wife and three children. He and his wife own a string of coffee shops located in medical centers in the Philadelphia area.

COLLEEN DELEGAN, a writer and producer, lives in Chicago. She spent five years in Europe and Asia, collecting material and traveling extensively. She has written pilots for NBC, CBS, and ABC in addition to several screenplays. In a previous life, Colleen was president of her own advertising agency, "Delegan & Kimmel, Words & Pictures," and was a creative director for Leo Burnett, U.S.A. Her first book, *Three Thousand Coffees in Vienna,* was published in 2004. She is currently under contract to ghostwrite a murder mystery.

PHILIP K. DICK was born in Chicago in 1928 and lived most of his life in California. In 1952, he began writing professionally and proceeded to write numerous novels and short-story collections. He won the Hugo Award for the best novel in 1962 for *The Man in the High Castle* and the John W. Campbell Memorial Award for best novel of the year in 1974 for *Flow My Tears, the Policeman Said.* He is most well-known for his short story "Do Androids Dream of Electric Sleep," made into the film *Blade Runner.* He died in 1982, shortly before the film was released. Dick was a prolific writer with forty-four novels and over one hundred short stories to his credit. Other film adaptations of his work include *Total Recall, A Scanner Darkly, Minority Report, Paycheck,* and *The Adjustment Bureau.*

BARBARA EKNOIAN's work has appeared in *PEARL, Chiron Review, Re)verb,* and *Cradle Song,* a motherhood anthology. She has received two Pushcart Prize nominations, and is a member of Donna Hilbert's poetry workshop in Long Beach, California. Her fiction was featured in the 2009 Sixth Annual Emerging Voices Show produced by Sally Shore's New Short Fiction Series. She hails from New Jersey and has never lost her accent.

DAN FANTE is the author of twelve books: Novels, poetry, plays, and short fiction. His work is published in eight languages. His new novel, the thriller *Point Doom,* will arrive in April 2013.

MERRILL FARNSWORTH is a Nashville-based writer, artist, and therapist. Born among the Texas tumbleweeds, Merrill came of age reveling in the sights and sounds of Puerto Rico's Afro-Caribbean culture. The cadences of South Carolina left their mark on her, as did melodies reaching from Appalachia to the Mississippi Delta. She is a published poet and award-winning lyricist, and recently collaborated with Phil Madeira on the Americana release *Mercyland.* In 2012, Silver Birch Press published *Jezebel's Got the Blues...And Other Works of Imagination,* Merrill's collection of performance pieces that was selected for 2012's The Puzzle, a festival of plays held in New York City. For more about Merrill, visit www.writingcircle.org.

SYED AFZAL HAIDER is a writer and founding editor of *Chicago Quarterly Review.* His short stories and essays have appeared in a variety of literary magazines including *Saint Ann's Review, AmerAsia, Rambunctious Review, The Journal of Pakistani Literature, The Taylor Trust, Trajectory, Marco Polo.* Indian Voices, Oxford University Press, Milkweed

Editions, Penguin Books, and Longman Literature have anthologized Haider. His short story collection, *Tumbleweed Connection,* was a finalist for the 2004 MVP competition. His first novel, *To Be With Her,* was published in 2010, and his second novel, *Life of Ganesh,* is forthcoming. He lives in Evanston, Illinois, with his wife and is father of two wonderful grown-up sons. He can be reached by email at sahaider@sbcglobal.net.

JOE HAKIM is a writer, poet, and spoken-word performer from Hull, East Yorkshire, U.K. He has performed at many venues and events around Britain, including Latitude Festival, Big Chill Festival, and the Edinburgh Fringe Festival. He is the co-organizer and host of "Write to Speak," a series of spoken-word events held at Hull Truck Theatre. His debut book, *No Light/Might Escape,* was published by Night Publishing. He recently wrote and directed his first play, *Blackout,* which was performed in September 2012 at Hull Truck Theatre as part of Greyscale Theatre's *Theatre Brothel 2.0.*

HENRY VIII was King of England from 1509 until his death in 1547. Best remembered for renouncing papal authority, establishing the Church of England, and his six marriages, Henry also found time to write—and was author of many songs and poems.

DONNA HILBERT's latest book, *The Green Season,* World Parade Books, a collection of poems, stories, and essays, is now available in an expanded second edition. Donna appears in and her poetry is the text of the documentary *Grief Becomes Me: A Love Story,* a Christine Fugate film. Earlier books include *Mansions* and *Deep Red* from Event Horizon, *Transforming Matter* and *Traveler in Paradise* from PEARL Editions, and the short story collection *Women Who Make Money and the Men Who Love Them* from Staple First Editions (published in England). Poems in Italian can be found in Bloc notes 59 and in French in *La page blanche,* in both cases translated by Mariacristina Natalia Bertoli. New work is in recent or forthcoming issues of *5AM, Nerve Cowboy, PEARL,* and *Poets & Artists.* A new collection, *The Congress of Luminous Bodies,* is forthcoming from Aortic Books. Learn more at www.donnahilbert.com.

GAIA HOLMES lives in Halifax, United Kingdom. She is a part-time creative writing lecturer at the University of Huddersfield and freelance writer who works with schools, libraries, and other community groups throughout the West Yorkshire region. In her spare time, Gaia is a DJ for Phoenix FM, the Borough of Calderdale's community radio station. She plays accordion with the band Crow Hill Stompers. Her second poetry collection, *Lifting the Piano with One Hand,* is scheduled for a Spring 2013 release from Comma Press.

GERARD MANLEY HOPKINS (1844-1889) was an English poet, Roman Catholic convert, and Jesuit priest. Most of his work was published posthumously and established him as one of the leading poets of the Victorian era. His use of "sprung rhythm" (a term he coined) and imagery established him as an innovator in a time when traditional verse was the norm. Many poets, including William Carlos Williams, Sylvia Plath, and Randall Jarrell, cite Hopkins as a major influence.

ZACK HUNTER is a synesthetic insomniac who loves nothing more than to explore the mysterious nature of our being. He was born in California after being implanted in a laboratory and has been writing ever since his first puff of cannabis at thirteen. He is the author of *Emily Virosa*, a novel.

RODGER JACOBS has won multiple awards and grants for his work as a journalist, documentary writer and producer, screenwriter, playwright, magazine editor, true crime writer, book critic and columnist for *PopMatters*, and live event producer. In 2010, he provided the preface and original inspiration for *Jack London: San Francisco Stories* (Sydney Samizdat Press). He is the author of the novel *The Furthest Palm,* published by Silver Birch Press in 2012.

JAMES JOYCE (1882-1941) was an Irish novelist considered by many critics to have written the greatest novel of all time, *Ulysses* (1922). Other works include *Dubliners* (1914), excerpted in this collection, *A Portrait of the Artist as a Young Man* (1916), and *Finnegans Wake* (1939). Joyce is known for his experimental use of language, extensive use of interior monologue, symbolism, and his puns, allusions, and invented words.

MICHAEL C. KEITH is the author of over twenty books on electronic media, among them *Talking Radio, Voices in the Purple Haze, Radio Cultures, Signals in the Air*, and the classic textbook *The Radio Station.* The recipient of numerous awards in his academic field, he is also the author of dozens of journal articles and short stories and has served in a variety of editorial positions. In addition, he is the author of an acclaimed memoir, *The Next Better Place,* a young adult novel, *Life is Falling Sideways*, and four story anthologies—*Of Night and Light, And Through the Trembling Air, Sad Boy,* and *Hoag's Object.* He has been nominated for a Pushcart Prize and Pen/O.Henry Award and was a finalist for the National Indie Excellence Award for short fiction anthology.

ERLE KELLY lives in Long Beach, California, and is a third-generation native of the Golden State. He attended California State University Long Beach, and the majority of his business career was in sales and marketing management. Erle is retired and his current interests are traveling with his wife, Kristine, gardening, cycling, and nature—and they are reflected in his poetry. He has been published in *New Verse News* and *Chiron Review* and belongs to a local poetry workshop conducted by Donna Hilbert. Erle also finds time to tutor students in reading and writing at a local elementary school in Long Beach. He finds poetry not only enriches his life but also the lives of the students he tutors.

RUTH MOON KEMPHER, an ex-navy brat who was born in Red Bank, New Jersey, has had her poetry and short prose appear in journals and other periodical publications since 1958, and has published many other people's work since 1994 through her Kings Estate Press in St. Augustine, Florida. She is retired from owning a tavern and from teaching—first for Flagler College while attaining her BA and graduating with the college's first class; and later, after achieving her MA at Emory University in Atlanta, in the English Department of St. Johns River Community College. The latest of her thirty-three (mostly small) collections of verse will also include prose pieces—*Key West Papers* is due from Casa de Cinco Hermanos Press, Pueblo, Colorado, in late 2012 or early 2013. After years of living at the beach, she now lives in the woods in an old cracker house with two dogs, Sadie, a long-legged hound, and Mister Frost, an emotional American Husky.

THOMAS KUDLA is a graduate of Indiana University, Bloomington. With the help of his tailored degree from the Individualized Major Program at IUB and a grant from the Indiana University Hutton Honors College, he was able to write his first novel, *Confessions of an American*. His book *What My Brain Told Me* was selected as a finalist in the short story nonfiction category of the 2009 National Indie Excellence Awards. For two years, Thom was an editor with the Sun-Times News Group. In 2011, he founded To a T Editorial Group, a manuscript editing business. To learn more about Thom, visit thomkudla.com.

STEVEN KUHN is a twenty-nine-year-old poet and photographer from Memphis, Tennessee. There, he works as an English teacher for Memphis City Schools and lives with his wife and a black-and-white rabbit named Charlie. He was recently featured in *The Bat Shat* poetry magazine, and is currently editing his first collection of poems, *Four Years in Pocket Change*. You can follow all his ramblings at his ill-maintained blog (steven-kuhn.blogspot.com) or contact him on Twitter @StevenKuhnPoet.

MORIAH LACHAPELL earned her bachelor's degree from Western Oregon University, studied Viticulture at Washington State University, and currently works in horticulture. An Oregon native and resident, she lives in a little town with her daughter and husband. Moriah has been published online and in print and is the editor of the online magazine *The Blue Hour* (thebluehour-magazine.com). You can visit her blog at moriahlachapell.wordpress.com.

LEEANNE MCILROY LANGTON is a Senior English Language Fellow for The U.S. Department of State and Georgetown University as well as a lecturer at California State University, Long Beach. A native Californian, she earned a BA in Linguistics from UCLA. and an MA in Linguistics from CSULB. In 2011, she was named "Most Valuable Professor" by the Honors Program at CSULB, where she also works as a faculty mentor for first-generation college students. She is the mother of two daughters.

ELLARAINE LOCKIE is a widely published and awarded poet, nonfiction book author, and essayist. Her ninth chapbook, *Wild as in Familiar,* was a finalist in the Finishing Line Press Chapbook contest and received *The Aurorean's* Chapbook Pick for Spring 2012. Ellaraine teaches poetry workshops and serves as poetry editor for the lifestyles magazine, *Lilipoh,* and as associate editor for *Mobius.* Silver Birch Press published her chapbook *Coffee House Confessions* in 2013.

GERALD LOCKLIN is a professor emeritus of English at California State University, Long Beach, where he taught full-time from 1965-2007, retains his office and contact information, and still teaches an occasional class as needed. He has published fiction, poetry, essays, and reviews prolifically in periodicals and in over a hundred and fifty books, chapbooks, and broadsides. Recent or upcoming books include a fiction e-Book, *The Sun Also Rises in the Desert,* from Mendicant Bookworks; a collection of poems, *Deep Meanings: Selected Poems, 2008-2013,* from PRESA Press; three simultaneously released novellas from Spout Press; and a French collection of his prose, *Candy Bars: Le Dernier des Damnes,* due May 7, 2013, from 13e Note Press, Paris. Event Horizon Press released new editions of *A Simpler Time, A Simpler Place* and *Hemingway Colloquium: The Poet Goes to Cuba* in 2011; Coagula Press released the first of two volumes of his *Complete Coagula Poems;* and *From a Male Perspective* appeared from PRESA Press. Reach him at gerlocklin@gmail.com, www.geraldlocklin.org, or www.facebook.com/geraldlocklin.

AMY LOWELL (1874-1925) was an American poet of the imagist school from Brookline, Massachusetts, who posthumously won the Pulitzer Prize for Poetry in 1926.

SANDYLEE MACCOBY has been a successful portrait painter and teacher of French and Spanish. As a child, she was a competitive figure skater and trained with world-renowned Gus Lussi. She retired from the sport at age thirteen. A graduate of Smith College, she is married to Michael Maccoby, PhD, a psychoanalyst and author, and lives in Washington, D.C.

TAMARA MADISON teaches English and French at a public high school in Los Angeles. Raised on a citrus farm in the California desert, Tamara's life has taken her many places, including Europe and the former Soviet Union, where she spent fifteen months in the 1970s. A swimmer and dog lover, Tamara says, "All I ever wanted to do with my life was write, and I mostly write poetry because it suits my lifestyle; I like the way one can say so much in the economical space of a poem."

MARC MALANDRA grew up primarily in Avalon, on Santa Catalina Island, California. He attended and has degrees from U.C. Santa Barbara, U.C. Davis, and Cornell University, where he received both an MFA in Creative Writing and a Ph.D. in English. Over the last twenty years, he has published poetry in approximately three dozen different venues, including *America*, *Cider Press Review*, *Flyway*, *Literature and Belief*, *Orange Coast Review*, *Poetry Northwest*, *Radix*, *South Florida Poetry Review*, and *Zocalo*. Currently Associate Professor of English and Director of the Writing Center at Biola University, he lives with his wife Junko, son Noah, and daughter Sasha in Brea, California.

KAREN MARGOLIS was born in Harare, Zimbabwe, and educated in South Africa and London. She graduated as a mathematician in 1974 and has since moved mainly in the world of words as a freelance author, poet, journalist, editor, broadcaster, and translator. She has lived in Berlin since 1983. Her books include *To Eat or Not to Eat* (1988), and *The Floating Castle* (Kindle 2012), and she has published poems and essays in numerous anthologies and magazines.

CLINT MARGRAVE lives in Long Beach, California. His first full-length collection of poems, *The Early Death of Men*, is newly released from NYQ Books. His work has also appeared or is forthcoming in *The New York Quarterly*, *Rattle*, *Ambit* (UK), *3AM* (UK), *PEARL*, *Serving House Journal*, *Word Riot*, and *Nerve Cowboy*, among others.

ANDREW MARVELL, born in England in 1621, was a poet as well as a politician who sat in the House of Commons. He belonged to the metaphysical school of poetry, where the writing often focused on love and faith. Marvell died in 1678 at age fifty-seven.

DANIEL MCGINN's work has appeared in the *OC Weekly*, *Next Magazine*, and other publications. His full-length collection of poems, *1000 Black Umbrellas*, is available from Write Bloody Press. He is currently a student in the low-residency MFA program at Vermont College of Fine Arts. He and his wife are natives of Southern California. They have three children, five grandchildren, and a very good dog.

LORI MCGINN is a mom, grandma, baker of cookies, visual artist, and writer of poems. A native of Whittier, California, her work has appeared in several anthologies and her chapbook, *Waiting*, was published as a part of the Laguna Poets Series.

MARCIA MEARA is a native Floridian living in the Orlando area with her husband of twenty-six years, two silly little dachshunds, and four big, lazy cats. She's fond of reading, gardening, hiking, canoeing, painting, and writing, not necessarily in that order. But her favorite thing in the world is spending time with her seven-year-old granddaughter, the world's funniest little girl. She and her husband are looking forward to the birth of their second grandchild in April 2013. Marcia is currently working on her first book, a romantic thriller set in the Blue Ridge Mountains, which she hopes will prove that it's never too late to follow your dream.

JACK MICHELINE was born in the East Bronx, New York, on November 6, 1929, as Harold Martin Silver. Informally educated, he identified closely with the traditions of American vagabond poets, such as Vachel Lindsay and Maxwell Bodenheim, and moved to Greenwich Village in the 1950s to find an outlet for his poetry. In 1958, Troubadour Press published his book, *River of Red Wine*, which was reviewed by Dorothy Parker in *Esquire*. Even though he proclaimed himself unaffiliated with any group, Micheline appeared frequently at poetry readings with Beat writers. He passed away in 1998.

BENJAMIN MYERS was born in Durham, United Kingdom, in 1976. His novels include *Pig Iron* (Bluemoose Books) and *Richard* (Picador). His stories, poems, articles, and interviews have appeared in numerous magazines, newspapers, and anthologies. He lives in Mytholmroyd, West Yorkshire, United Kingdom. Find him at his online blog by visiting www.benmyersmanofletters.blogspot.com.

BROOKE NIA has been a featured poet at some of the most prestigious venues in Los Angeles, including Beyond Baroque Literary Arts Center, Highways Performance Space and Gallery, the World Stage Performance Gallery, and the Mark Taper Forum in the Los Angeles Central Library as a part of the Newer Poets XIII Reading, and many more. She received the 2008 World Stage UCLA Scholarship and is published in Pearl Magazine. Brooke credits the World Stage and Jawanza Dumisani as the preeminent influences in the development of her work.

JAX NTP is a graduate student at Cal State Long Beach in the Masters of Fine Arts, Creative Writing Program. Her poetry has been featured on KBeach Radio, *Moon Tide Press*, *Subliminal Interiors*, and *The Más Tequila Review*. She is editor-in-chief of CSULB's Literary Journal, *RipRap* Volume 35. "Medusa Sonata" won The Aquarium of the Pacific's 3rd Annual Urban Ocean Poetry Festival in May 2012.

IVON PREFONTAINE is a junior high teacher in a small satellite community of Edmonton, Alberta, Canada. He regained an appreciation for poetry and found his way back to it after many years. Poetry has reemerged as an integral aspect of his personal expression and complements a growing meditative practice.

JONNE RHODES writes and lives near the edge of the Bolsa Chica wetlands in Southern California. She recently reconnected and is an active participant in Donna Hilbert's Poetry Workshop. She finds inspiration in nature, family, and past experience as a Montessori teacher, art instructor, and ESL tutor.

CONRAD ROMO grew up on the other side of the tracks in L.A., short, stocky, and swarthy. He is the producer and host of one of the very best literary reading events in L.A.—Tongue & Groove at the Hotel Café, now in its ninth year. Each month, he blends a handpicked mix of writers to present short fiction, poetry, personal essays, along with a musical guest. His writing has appeared in *Los Angeles Review, Wednesday Magazine, Noveltown, Tu Ciudad, Brooklyn & Boyle, Palehouse, Huizache,* and *Latinos in Lotusland.* Visit Conrad at the Tongue & Groove website: tongueandgroovela.com.

LUKE SALAZAR—Thwarting Your Efforts Since 1972. Luke has worked as a repoman, database guru, forklift driver, and licensed private investigator…but never all at once. He holds an MFA in Creative Writing from California State University, Long Beach, and currently works as an editor at a newswire—sprinkling hyphens and commas into poorly written corporate press releases. Luke's poetry can be found in publications such as *PEARL, Ambit* (UK), *The Ledge, Chiron Review, Re)verb, Spot Lit Magazine, MEAT Magazine* (UK), the Silver Birch Press *Silver Anthology,* and more. In October 2012, Aortic Press published *California Burning,* Luke's first full-length collection of poetry. For a cranial field trip, visit lukesalazar.com.

TERE SIEVERS, originally a Jersey girl, lives in Long Beach, California, and works as a Marriage and Family Therapist. She began writing poetry at CSULB and Beyond Baroque back in the late '70s. For the enjoyment of the children in her life, she has published a book of children's poems, *Blueberry Pancakes and Monkey Pajamas.* She recently received third place in the *Your Daily Poem* Apocalypse Poetry Contest.

JOAN JOBE SMITH, founding editor of *PEARL* and *Bukowski Review,* worked for seven years as a go-go dancer before receiving her BA from CSULB and MFA from University of California, Irvine. A Pushcart Honoree, her award-winning work has appeared internationally in more than five hundred publications, including *Outlaw Bible, Ambit, Beat Scene, Wormwood Review,* and *Nerve Cowboy*—and she has published twenty collections, including *Jehovah Jukebox* (Event Horizon Press, US) and *The Pow Wow Cafe* (The Poetry Business, UK), a finalist for the

UK 1999 Forward Prize. In July 2012, with her husband, poet Fred Voss, she did her sixth reading tour of England (debuting at the 1991 Aldeburgh Poetry Festival), featured at the Humber Mouth Literature Festival in Hull. In November 2012, Silver Birch Press published her literary profile entitled *Charles Bukowski Epic Glottis: His Art & His Women (& me)*. In 2013, World Parade Books will release her memoir *Tales of an Ancient Go-Go Girl*. Her literary magazine *PEARL* will release its fiftieth edition in 2013—find out more at pearlmag.com.

CLIFTON SNIDER, faculty emeritus at Cal State University, Long Beach, is the internationally acclaimed author of ten books of poetry. A career retrospective of his work, *Moonman: New and Selected Poems*, was published by World Parade Books (2012). His novel about the rise, fall, and physical and spiritual recovery and comeback of a 1980s bisexual rock star, *Loud Whisper* (2000), has been optioned by Iconoclastic Features. His coming out/coming-of-age novel, *Bare Roots,* was published in 2001, as was his novel about two gay Pentecostal preacher's sons, *Wrestling with Angels: A Tale of Two Brothers*. A Jungian/Queer literary critic, his book, *The Stuff That Dreams Are Made On,* was published in 1991, and he has published hundreds of poems, fiction, reviews, and articles internationally. His work has been translated into French. Spanish, and Russian.

DALE SPROWL teaches writing at Biola University in La Mirada, California. During summers, she administrates and teaches at the Young Writer's Project at UCI. Her work with the UCI Writing Project began in 1981, and she has contributed to the UCIWP texts on the teaching of writing. Her first chapbook of poems, *The Colors of Water,* published by Finishing Line Press in 2007, and her second chapbook, *Moon Over Continent's Edge (*2009), have been nominated for a California Book Award. Her poems have also appeared in *PEARL, Fire, A New Song, Ancient Paths,* and *Knowing Stones: Poems of Exotic Places*. She earned her bachelor's degree in humanities and in history as well as a master's degree in history from Pepperdine University. An Educator Associate for the American Psychoanalytic Association, she lives in Newport Beach, California, with her husband.

KENDALL STEINLE grew up in Akron, Ohio. She attended Saint Xavier University in Chicago, along with a stint at the University of Glasgow, receiving her Bachelor's in English with minors in Writing and Middle Eastern Studies. Her first publication was in *Journal of Microliterature*. She is currently pursuing her master's degree in Writing and Publishing at DePaul University.

TATE SWINDELL is a poet, painter, photographer, and filmmaker. His record label, Unrequited Records, has released readings from Herbert

Huncke, Harold Norse, and Jack Micheline. Tate and Todd Swindell are currently working on a film about Harold Norse, pulling from their numerous hours of footage shot at the poet's historic Mission flat in San Francisco. After a decade spent on the frontlines of the medical cannabis movement, Tate is committed to evolution through art.

PAUL KAREEM TAYYAR, a three-time nominee for the Pushcart Prize, is the author of four collections of poetry: *Everyday Magic* (West-Coast Bias Press), *Scenes From A Good Life* (Tebot Bach), *Postmark Atlantis* (Level 4 Press), and *Follow the Sun: Poems, Stories, and Reflections* (Aortic Books). Paul's most recent book of prose is the novella *In the Footsteps of the Silver King* (Spout Hill Press). He is the Founding Director of World Parade Books, an independent press that has published works by Edward Field, Clifton Snider, and Donna Hilbert. He is one of the organizers of Beside the City of Angels: A Long Beach Poetry Festival.

G. MURRAY THOMAS has been an active part of the SoCal poetry scene for over twenty years. *News Clips & Ego Trips*, a collection of articles from *Next* was just published by Write Bloody Press. His most recent book of poetry is *My Kidney Just Arrived*, published by Tebot Bach in 2011. His previous books are *Cows on the Freeway* and *Paper Shredders*, an anthology of surf writing. For more, visit: gmurraythomas.com.

JERI THOMPSON, a former creative writing major who studied with Elliott Fried and Gerald Locklin at California State University, Long Beach, is currently a blogger (at Trikker Chicks...For Women Who Carve) and regular contributor to *TrikkeWorld* magazine. She can often be found walking around downtown Long Beach in bright blue Pumas or riding on a Trikke (with two Ks).

MARGARET TOWNER is a teacher of English learners and students at-risk in reading. She lived for many years in Latin America—Uruguay, Chile, El Salvador, and Mexico—and translates poetry from Spanish to English, writes children's music, and performs Latin American music. In 2005, she received the Jane Buel Bradley Chapbook Award, and her poetry will be featured in the *Cancer Poetry Project Anthology*, the Serving House Press, and the Center for Nondual Awareness.

MARY UMANS is a filmmaker and writer living in New York City. Her short film, *The Braddock Boys*, was featured in the 2012 Manhattan Film Festival.

PHILIP VERMAAS lives in Cape Town, South Africa, at the moment. He's a professional copywriter, published poet and writer, and excessive drinker. At some point during any given day, you can find him editing the online poetry magazine *Misfits' Miscellany*. He used to believe he would never be very good at life, now he knows he was right. Money eludes him and for a long while he stopped believing in love, but now he believes in love again. He is not sure if he believes in anything else. An extract from his novel *Nourishment* can be read in the cult pulp South African magazine *Jungle Jim.*

DIRK VELVET is a Poet/Writer of Songs from Muskego, Wisconsin. His writing has been featured in *Beggars and Cheeseburgers, PEARL, Re)verb, Nerve Cowboy,* and *Milwaukee Renaissance.*

MELANIE VILLINES is a novelist, playwright, screenwriter, television writer, biographer, editor, and ghostwriter. Her published work includes the novel *Tales of the Sacred Heart* (Bogfire Press), the family memoir *Reason to Fight* (co-written with Hiram Johnson), a celebrity biography *Beyond Hollywood* (co-written with J. Herbert Klein), *Anna & Otto*, a novel for children (Inklings Press), and a variety of ghostwritten books and screenplays. Her play *Bernice* (co-written with Hiram Johnson) had a recent workshop production in Dallas.

KURT VONNEGUT (1922-2007) was born in Indianapolis, Indiana, and attended Cornell University before serving in the U.S. Army during World War II, where as a prisoner of war he witnessed the bombing of Dresden, Germany—an experience that became the basis for his masterwork, the 1969 novel *Slaughterhouse-Five.*. After World War II, Vonnegut studied Anthropology at the University of Chicago and served as a police reporter for the Chicago News Bureau. He later worked as a publicist for General Electric in Schenectady, New York, before leaving to become a full-time writer. While establishing his career, Vonnegut wrote short stories for pulp magazines, as evidenced by the story ("2 B R 0 2 B") included in this collection. In addition to *Slaughterhouse-Five*, Vonnegut's novels include *Player Piano* (1952), *Mother Night* (1961), *Cat's Cradle* (1971), *Breakfast of Champions* (1973), *Slapstick* (1976), *Deadeye Dick* (1982), *Gallapagos* (1985), *Bluebeard* (1987), *Hocus Pocus* (1990), and *Timequake* (1997).

FRED VOSS, a machinist for thirty-two years, has had three collections of poetry published by the U.K.'s Bloodaxe Books. He is regularly published in magazines such as *Poetry Review* (London), *Ambit* (London), *Rising* (London), *The Shop* (Ireland), *Atlanta Review,* and *PEARL*, and has twice been the subject of feature programs about his poetry on National BBC Radio 4. In 2008, he was featured at The Ledbury Poetry Festival, and in 2011 he and his wife, poet Joan Jobe Smith, were featured readers at the University of Pittsburgh and, in 2012 were featured at The Humber Mouth Literature Festival (Hull, England). His latest book, *Hammers and Hearts of the Gods* from Bloodaxe Books, was selected by U.K. newspaper *The Morning Star* as one of the Top Seven Books for 2009. In 2011, he was featured poet in a hardbound limited edition of *DWANG* (London, England), and in 2013 World Parade Books will publish his first novel, *Making America Strong.*

BRUCE WEIGL entered the Army at eighteen and served in Vietnam for one year, beginning in December 1967. He was awarded the Bronze Star and returned to his hometown of Lorain, Ohio, where he enrolled in Lorain County Community College. He earned his BA at Oberlin College, his MA at the University of New Hampshire, and his PhD at the University of Utah. Weigl is the author of more than a dozen books of poetry, including *The Unraveling Strangeness* (2002), *Archeology of the Circle: New and Selected Poems* (1999), and *After the Others* (1999). He has also written several collections of critical essays, has published translations of Vietnamese and Romanian poetry, and has also edited or co-edited several anthologies of war poetry, including *Writing Between the Lines: An Anthology on War and Its Social Consequences* (1997) and *Mountain River: Vietnamese Poetry from the Wars, 1948–1993; A Bilingual Collection* (1998). Weigl's poetry has been widely anthologized, including in *Best American Poetry* (1994), *The Morrow Anthology of Younger American Poets* (1985), *Against Forgetting: Twentieth Century Poetry of Witness* (1993), and *American Alphabets: 25 Contemporary Poets* (2006). Weigl has won the Robert Creeley Award, the Lannan Literary Award for Poetry, the Paterson Poetry Prize, the Poet's Prize from the Academy of American Poets, the Cleveland Arts Prize, and two Pushcart Prizes. *Song of Napalm* (1998) was nominated for the Pulitzer Prize. He has also been awarded fellowships from the National Endowment for the Arts and the Yaddo Foundation.

TIM WELLS likes reggae, beer, and pie 'n' mash. He lives in East London, United Kingdom.

PAMELA MILLER WOOD, a native Californian, has lived in the Los Angeles area most of her life. For over thirty years, she has enjoyed a successful career in the Southern California real estate industry, garnering many awards for outstanding achievement along the way, including Top Producer in Los Angeles County for ten consecutive years. *Charles Bukowski's Scarlet* is Pam's first full-length book—a memoir of her multi-year relationship with legendary author Charles Bukowski—a true tour de force.

EDDIE WOODS, born in 1940 in New York City, is a widely traveled poet and prose writer who has variously worked as a short-order cook, computer programmer, encyclopedia salesman, restaurant manager, and journalist. In his youth, he spent four years in the U.S. Air Force to avoid being drafted into the Army (didn't want to get his fingernails dirty!), as well as to breathe the sexually free air of Europe. After living in many other parts of the world, since 1978 he has mainly resided in Amsterdam, the Netherlands. His website is http://eddiewoods.nl.

www.ingramcontent.com/pod-product-compliance
Lightning Source LLC
Chambersburg PA
CBHW071458170626
46811CB00007B/2617